METANOIA

A Transformational Journey

METANOIA

A Transformational Journey

Mary Ogden Davis

DeVorss & Company
Box 550
Marina del Rey, California, 90294–0550

Printed in the United States of America

About the Cover . . .

Standing on the waters of the infinite cosmic mind stuff, the cup symbolizes the body of mankind. The sun rising from the cup is symbolic of the God-like nature of man coming into being through the manifestation of his mortal form. The rising sun also symbolizes repeated renewal with blessings to come from this new start.

To meditate on this picture is to meditate on wealth in things of the Spirit as well as of earth. It is to meditate on abundance, beauty, love, joy and a new beginning.

Cover design by Berlyn J. Erdahl

Grateful Acknowledgment to:

My beloved church youth group, the Neophytes, and to the world's greatest study group, the Hi-Nooners, for whom these lessons were originally prepared.

My son Michael, who gave me much needed technical assistance and encouragement, and would accept nothing less than technical excellence.

Linda Kolich, who made sense out of my notes, deletions and additions as she typed the pages into manuscript form.

Norman Brekke for his careful, thoughtful and thorough editing.

Trina Capka, who did the initial typing into the word processor and helped with the first proofreading.

Berlyn Erdahl, whose art work on the cover so beautifully interprets the essence of this work.

All of my friends who read and, with eagle-eye, proofread the first printing.

My husband John for his loving support and helpful suggestions.

My family, who gave me the space to read and research, and write and rewrite.

Religious Science, and to its founder, Ernest Holmes, for the five steps of Spiritual Mind Treatment used in this book as chapter headings: Recognition, Unification, Realization, Thanksgiving, and Release.

The dedicated, illumined men and women of both the past and present that have made the way so much easier with their insight, their teaching, their books.

Jesus, the Christ, who brought a new dispensation, a new energy to our planet; who taught and lived the Truth that sets us free.

To all who helped make this book possible, Thank you very much!

Preface

The Transformational Journey is a story of Self-Discovery. There is nothing new in this story, only old truths retold. But these truths are of such vivid and perennial interest that, though old, they are never stale. And though well known, there is always something to say which seems to throw on them new light and new meaning, for they bring us in touch with ourselves.

Contents

Foreword

Metanoia (Greek), the New Testament word for repentance, means "change of mind." It refers to the willingness to change, to be submissive to the Father's loving Will and to remove whatever is an obstacle to loving relationship with Him. Actually, we do not have any one English word which adequately expresses the New Testament meaning of metanoia. "Repentance," which is commonly used, means "to be sorry again" (from the Latin "repoenitet") rather than a change of thought and purpose, a mental revolution which affects the course of one's life.

In Romans 12:2, St. Paul exhorts us to:

Be not conformed to this world: but be ye transformed by the renewing of your mind, that ye may prove what is that good, and acceptable, and perfect will of God.

The "metanoia" experience is the "born again" experience; we are "*A new creature and old things are passed away: Behold all things are become new!*" II Corinthians 5:17

1

The Journey Begins

The Preparation . . . Lent

The transformational journey of everyone is told in the Gospel biography of Jesus the Christ. Every person is a potential manifest Christ, and the unfolding of the Christ-life in each one follows the outline of the Gospel Story. It is quite certain that Jesus, as the way-shower, passed through every stage which we must go through if we would be "on the path".

Jesus said, If thou will be perfect, come follow thou Me. Matthew 19:21

We take the Bibical story of Jesus the Christ to be a fact in history, but it is also an allegory. The purpose of an allegory is not to relate concrete facts and events which take place in time and space; it is rather to symbolize certain realities beyond time and space, realities of the divine and eternal order.

As we teach our children by means of stories and pictures, truths that they are not mature enough to grasp, so the spiritual leaders of mankind have used "teaching stories" to pass on hidden information and power down through the ages. Thus, the teaching story, such as the allegories and parables of the Bible, preserves priceless information.

The Easter story has meaning for us all if we read the message beyond the words. It is impossible to follow Jesus through the steps leading to the crucifixion and the resurrection without having some sort of revelation in ourselves.

We can identify with Jesus because we are spiritually one with Him, as we are one with each other. His love is our love. Whatever we love and think on, that we become. So by loving Jesus and the Christ Principle, and by following in His steps to the best of our ability, we become like Him.

Each event in the life of Jesus the Christ is a definite fact in the experience of every sincere follower of Truth. Each step is known as an "initiation." An initiation is simply an expansion of consciousness—a stage of illumination.

Though we find all kinds of resemblances between the Christ story, the seasons, the growth cycle of nature, and the myths of gods who were ancient when Jesus was born, the Christ Story is not some survival

of old superstitions. For the CHRIST IS THE EMBODI-
MENT, OR INCARNATION, OF THE WORD OF
GOD. The WORD means the ideal pattern or divine
law by which and in accordance with which the universe and (generic) man are created. Since the WORD
is the design in the Mind of the Architect of the Universe, there is every reason to expect resemblances between the life of Jesus and the processes of nature as
they are found in the heavens, in man, and in life on
this earth.

For more then fifteen hundred years, the Festival of
Easter has celebrated the resurrection of Jesus the
Christ. But not only is the very name "Easter" the
name of an ancient and non-Christian deity, the season
itself has always been the occasion of rites and observances associated with the mystery of death and resurrection among people differing widely in race and
religion.

The word *Easter* was originally the name of an An-
glo-Saxon goddess of the dawn, known as Eostre, or
Ostare, whose principal festival was kept at the vernal
equinox. The date of Easter is from the vernal equinox:
that is, from the beginning of spring, when, after the
long nights of winter, day and night are equal again
before the lengthening days of summer. Equinox (equal
night) is the time when the sun's center crosses the

equator and day and night are everywhere of equal length, around the 21st day of March. Vernal means appearing, or coming, in the spring.

There is an annual "journey" of the sun corresponding to its daily "journey" from noon to noon through sunset, night and dawn. Dawn would correspond to the vernal equinox, so there is always a connection between sunrise and spring.

The date of Easter changes every year, and may indeed come at any time between March 22 and April 25. The reason for the changing date is not only that Easter day must always be on a Sunday, since Christ rose on the first day of the week; but also, it is determined by both the solar and the lunar calendars. Easter is the Sunday following the first full moon after the vernal equinox. The lunar calendar is used together with the solar calendar because, at the time of Jesus, the Jews measured their months by the moon.

A multitude of popular customs, many of which survive among us today, are derived from the Christian Easter Story, from the rites of the church, and from pagan observances which existed in Europe long before Christian times.

The Easter Egg is not the most important thing about Easter, but it is certainly the first memory of Easter most of us have from childhood. In American folklore, the Easter Egg is the production not of some mystical bird, but of a rabbit, a tradition from Central and Western Europe

Hindu mythology tells us of the World-Egg which was formed in the Waters of Chaos before the universe and time had begun.

In modern America, the one Easter custom that appears to be really universal is the donning of new clothes at Easter time. But the crowds who join in Easter parades dressed in their new finery, are probably unaware that they represent a last dim survival of the conferring of white robes upon the newly baptized.

It is commonly believed that the Lenten period has to do with the events of the forty days preceding the resurrection. Lent, derived from an Old English word for spring meaning, "to lengthen," is a church institution with no authority anywhere in the New Testament. Lent begins on Ash Wednesday, forty days before Easter, excluding Sundays, and ends on Easter Sunday.

Since Lent is a period of preparation for Easter, the idea apparently was based on the forty-day period of prayer and fasting as practiced by Moses, Elijah and Jesus. Moses received the Ten Commandments on Mount Sinai at the conclusion of his forty-day fast. Elijah talked with God on Mount Horeb at the conclusion of his forty days of prayer and fasting. Jesus began His ministry at the close of His forty-day fast in the wilderness.

The ancient Hebrew writers made a practice of using numbers to symbolize ideas. Forty, in their minds, was a "foursquare" number suggesting the idea of a foundation for something to follow.

The present idea of observing the forty days of Lent was unknown in the early church. They had a celebration of forty hours, not forty days. It was calculated that the body of Jesus lay in the sepulchre about forty hours. It was thought by many early Christians that those hours preceding the celebration of the Resurrection should be observed as a time of prayer and fasting.

We can think of prayer as a communion between God and man, the affirmation of Spiritual Truths that have not yet come into manifestation, a disciplined opening of self to God. To fast is to abstain from negative thinking. It can also be thought of as denial. The word "deny" has two definitions according to Webster. To deny, in one sense, is to "withhold from." But to deny in another sense is "to declare to be not true, to repudiate as utterly false."

We should deny the appearance of evil, affirm good; deny weakness, affirm strength. Through our spoken (and thought) word, we are continually making the world in which we live. All through the Bible we find an empahsis on the importance of words.

In the beginning was the Word, and the Word was with God, and the Word was God, and the Word was made flesh, and dwelt among us.

John 1:1 & 14

But I say unto you, that every idle word that men shall speak, they shall give account thereof in the day of judgment. For by thy words thou shalt be justified and by thy words thou shalt be condemned. Mathew 12:36 & 37

So shall My word be that goeth forth out of My mouth; it shall not return unto Me void, but shall accomplish that which I please, and it shall prosper in the thing whereto I sent it. Isaiah 55:11

Hebrews bound upon their foreheads and wrists, parchments with words of Scripture written upon them. The Hindus, Japanese, Chinese, and the people of nearly all other known nations, have their various ways of applying the sacred words to aid them in both their material and spiritual needs.

Many people are intellectually persuaded of the Truth, yet do not get results through their knowledge. What is needed is to bathe this knowledge in the deep feeling of Truth. It is the emotion (energy in motion) that impresses the word on the subjective.

As a man thinketh in his heart, so is he.

Proverbs 23:7

The "heart" in metaphysics is interpreted to be the subjective, the seat of the emotions. We are told in the Bible that we must be "in agreement". This means that the conscious and the subjective mind must be saying the same thing. There must be the word (spoken or thought) and the emotion, the warmth, the feeling. This could be likened to the seed planted in the earth, warmed by the rays of the sun. The manifestation (plant) is the natural result as we "let go and let God." We cannot "make" a demonstration happen anymore than we can "make" a seed sprout and grow.

Every word we speak (think) is a creative word, but it is the feeling that the word expresses and which accompanies it that subjectifies it. To think and speak the Truth clearly and with feeling leads to the demonstrations we desire. As long as treatment (prayer) is kept on an intellectual level, there is no demonstration. Our attention and emotion energize our words and thoughts. Feelings are the vehicle; thoughts are the passengers. It is the emotion (energy in motion), the feeling, that impresses the word on the subjective.

Feeling is not merely an involuntary process, as many people believe. It is part of the activity of will. Will can be used to arouse feeling. By an act of will we speak our word. By an act of will we can control our emotions. Too often, when we talk about our troubles, we are full of feeling. But when words of Truth are spoken, the second pole, emotion, is missing.

Gratitude is a dynamic emotion. We are admonished in Ephesians 5:20 to:

Give thanks always for all things unto God!

And in Philippians 4:6 to:

Be careful for nothing, but in everything by prayer and supplication with thanksgiving let your requests be made known to God.

The seed of thanksgiving with our prayer request is an affirmation of God's return to us.

And Jesus lifted up his eyes, and said, "Father, I thank thee that thou hast heard me. And I know that thou hearest me always"   John 11:41 & 42

Enthusiasm, from the Greek word *ethos*, means "full of God," Enthusiasm is a magnet that attracts all the good things to us. Gratitude, thanksgiving, and enthusiasm lead to joy. Joy is an expression of God as life.

The joy of the Lord is your strength. Nehemia 8:10

Let them that love Thy name be Joyful in Thee
                                                Psalms 5:11

Make a joyful noise unto God all ye lands.
                                                Psalms 66:1

When we are joyous, we are, by our very actions, blessing and praising everything about us. We have the conviction, the faith, of God's continuous care.

Faith is an inner sureness, a confident expectancy. Faith is a spiritual force. The prayer of faith is given us in Mark 11:22, 24:

And Jesus answering saith unto them, "Have faith in God.

Therefore, I say unto you, what things soever ye desire, when ye pray, believe that ye (already) receive them, and ye shall have them."

In legal terms, "shall" means just that—absolutely! Faith is acting on the word. Faith is doing something about what we say we believe. Faith is "digging our ditches," (II Kings 15) preparing to receive. When we prepare to receive, take the necessary steps, the evidence manifests in the physical world in a very natural way. But even before there is any sign, since by faith we believe that we have received, we say, "Thank you,

Father, I believe that I have received." Faith instinctively works through the emotion (energy in motion) of gratitude.

So right where we are in our lives, we put ourselves there with our words and our emotions. We are the product of what we've been saying with our mouths and believing in our hearts.

For with the heart, man believeth unto righteousness; and with the mouth confession is made unto salvation. Romans 10:10

With the heart we believe, with the mouth we confess. To confess means to acknowledge, recognize as a fact, as one's own. Faith is released by words.

Through faith we understand that the worlds are framed by the word of God so that things which are seen are not made of things which do appear. Hebrews 11:3

However, St. Paul declares in I Corinthians 13:2 & 13

If I have all faith so that I could remove mountains and have not love, I am nothing.

And now abideth faith, hope, love, these three; but the greatest of these is love.

To love is to put ourselves in harmony with the universe.

God is love, and he that dwelleth in love dwelleth in God, and God in him.   I John 4:16

We are told in I Corinthians 16:14, to *Let all your things be done with love.* When we do all that we do in love, we become the vehicle through which life lives itself. We know that we are no longer living our life, but that the Presence and The Power is living as each one of us. Be sure that there is nothing but love in your thoughts for God, for man, and for your work before you begin any special task. This is to put God into it, which means power for the execution and perfection in the result.

Bless the Lord, oh my soul, and all that is within me, bless His holy name!   Psalms 103:1

The love, the adoration, the high praise that we send forth from our heart into the world is perfected and multiplied by the action of the Christ Mind.

In the Lord's Prayer, *Hallowed be Thy name,* (Matthew 6:9) is the adoration of God. The word "hallowed" has the same meaning as holy, whole, complete. In the Bible, as elsewhere, the "name" of anything means the essential nature or character of that thing. So the nature of God is complete and perfect, is entire.

It is at this point, the adoration of God, that we stay until we feel the warmth, the love of God filling us, untill we feel the light from the I AM Presence flooding our entire being.

We contemplate the nature of God. God is all in all; is all-knowing, all-powerful, ever-present. God is Love, God is Wisdom, God is Abundance, God is Life, God is Harmony, God is Truth, and I AM That! And now God's joy comes bubbling up and fills every cell of the body, every atom of the being.

Jesus gave us the commandment of intense devotion, the prayer of the heart, in Mark 12:30:

Thou shalt love the Lord thy God with all thy heart, and with all thy soul, and with all thy mind, and with all thy strength; this is the first commandment.

This prayer of the heart allows anyone who uses it fully to become open and ready to live in the ebb and flow of God's will.

Finally, brethren, whatsoever things are true, whatsoever things are honest, whatsoever things are lovely, whatsoever things are of good report; if there be any virtue, and if there be any praise, think on these things. Philippians 4:8

Here and now is the time for "prayer and fasting." A preparation for that which is to come, the *Christ in you, the hope of glory.* Colossians 1:27

2

The First Initiation

The Birth . . . *Recognition*

There is no individual with more God presence than another, yet there is a greater degree of awareness of the Presence in one than in another. This brings us to the first initiation, RECOGNITION. We must recognize and become aware of the indwelling Christ Principle within us. This is the first stage in the unfolding of the Life of Love; it is spoken of as the "Birth," and the Christmas Story represents this first expansion of consciousness.

At this stage, we know that God is within, that God is immanent. A God as transcendent only, suggests a God as above and beyond His creation. This idea of God as remote from the practical affairs of man or from man's own experience is false.

God is "closer than breathing, nearer than hands and feet." At this stage we know the ISness of God. God is NOW! God is right where we are. God in the absolute is everywhere present, but God in the particular is only at the point of Recognition.

The process of evolving from sense to soul to Spirit is first of all a RECOGNITION of our Spiritual Self-hood. Jesus said, *I and My Father are one.* John 10:30

At this stage, the Christ, this immanent God, this indwelling presence, becomes very real, very warm and very personal. Never again will God seem far off, unavailable and uninterested. We reach this place, "The Birth," when, either through wisdom or because of suffering, we are prepared to really put God first.

When Isaiah was prophesying the Birth of Jesus the Christ, he said:

> *For unto us a child is born, unto us a son is given:*
> *and the government shall be upon his shoulders*
> *and his name shall be called wonderful, counselor,*
> *the mighty God, the everlasting Father, the Prince*
> *of Peace.* Isaiah 9:6

The Child, of course, is the Truth, the Christ within—and the Government shall be upon His shoulders when He is born in us, when we acknowledge Him. This means that when once we have contacted the mystic power within, and have allowed it to take over our responsibilities for us, it will direct and govern all our affairs from the greatest to the least without effort, without mistakes, and without trouble to us.

The name of anything in the Bible means the character or nature of that thing. The name of the Child is

"Wonderful." As soon as this Child takes over in our life our troubles disappear. Another name is "counselor." A counselor gives advice or guidance. The Child is our infallible counselor—never makes a mistake. Another name is God Himself, the "Mighty God." The Child, the Christ, is one with God. The Child is called the "Prince of Peace," It is the very nature of the Child to give us soul peace.

And how shall we recognize Truth? How can we know if the Christ "though wrapped in swaddling clothes, lying in a manger," is being born in our hearts? Simply this: if the Christ is to be born in our hearts, we must be living the life of the Christ; we must show forth His Spirit to those around us. The Christ Spirit is first of all Love and Brotherhood.

The person in whom the Christ is developing will certainly express love, kindliness, tolerance, comprehension, an increase of the quality which for want of a better word we often call "bigness." This person would not be concerned about his own little feelings, would not be over-sensitive.

If we are developing the Christ within us, we would begin to take the best view of people and of things, instead of the worst. We would make a practice of putting the best construction possible upon the words and actions of everyone instead of the worst possible.

If we were in a position to get behind the thought of

the person and find out really why he did or said a certain thing, we would probably find that we were incorrect and unjust in our judging, that he had some thought in mind which never even occurred to us. A person in whom the "Birth" is taking place does not criticize unnecessarily, but would see the good.

In Luke 2:13 we read:

And suddenly there was with the angel, a multitude of the heavenly host praising God, and saying, "Glory to God in the highest, and on earth peace, good will toward men!"

This is the key to the mental attitude in which the Christ Consciousness is born in us—while we are praising God. This cannot be said too often, while we are praising and glorifying. The Christ is not born in us when we are criticizing, complaining, worried, angry, frightened, or wishing someone ill. The Christ is born in us when we are praising good! Through praising and recognizing the Christ, we arrive at Bethlehem, the abiding place of substance. The Divine Law is SPIRITUAL RECOGNITION AND PRAISE.

This, in brief, is the eternal message of Christmas. It is also the first Initiation. The meaning is that the Christ, the Sonship of God, is within each one of us—waiting only to be recognized.

The first initiation, recognition, is chiefly concerned with the conquering of the belief of separation. Now God is personal to us; God is immanent; God is indwelling.

And they shall call His name, Emmanuel, which being interpreted is, God with us.   Matthew 1:23

At this stage, of great comfort to us is the simple affirmation, "God is with me." One of the boys in a youth group told of driving down a mountain late at night from a camping trip. He was tired and sleepy and nervous. The other boys were all asleep. The steering wheel seemed to be jiggling and hard to handle. He remembered our talking in class about using the affirmation, "God is with me" in times of stress when nothing else would come to mind. All at once he relaxed, the steering wheel quit jiggling, and in a very short time they were safely out of the mountains.

When we wish to share that which is most real or most sacred with another person, we have a "heart-to-heart" talk with him. In this same way, we seek a relationship with God, especially under great stress, which is heart-to-heart.

Our need is not satisfied by the Lord of Hosts, nor do we find contentment in the splendor and majesty or power of the Divine Mind, or in the law of cause and effect. We long for the simple assurance of God's love.

This deep need within us for love is actually a need to overcome our feeling of separation—to leave our prison of aloneness, to reach out and unite ourselves in some form or other with other people, with the world outside.

Yet, often we practice daily the belief in separation without ever being aware of it. Good will is unity; ill will is separation. Love and acceptance are unity; nagging and criticism are separation. Laughter is unity; tears are separation. Faith is unity; despair is separation. Generous congratulation is unity; silent envy is separation. Trust is unity; jealousy is separation.

Dr. Frederick Bailes, in *HIDDEN POWER FOR HUMAN PROBLEMS*, writes that the "parent thought" underlying the accident habit is that of separation. The parent thought of separation operates in other fields as well. It brings about jiltings, desertions, loss of jobs, broken friendships, and a host of other situations in which one becomes separated from that to which he wishes (consciously) to remain attached.

And Dr. Flanders Dunbar, well-known exponent of psychosomatic medicine, maintains that the thought patterns of the accident-prone person and of the criminal are similar. The one unconsciously takes it out on society. The other unconsciously punishes himself through accidents. The consequences too are similar. One suffers separation from society in prison, the other in a hospital, with fractures, dislocations, or torn ligaments—all of which are separations.

The belief of separation from God, without reunion by love, is the source of our anxiety, our grief, our miseries. Sickness is a belief of separation from health; poverty is a belief of separation from supply; loneliness is a belief of separation from love, and so it goes—this feeling of being separated from our Good, from our God.

However, St. Paul writes in Romans 8:35, 37–39 that we cannot be separated.

Who shall separate us from the love of Christ? Shall tribulation, or distress, or persecution, or famine, or nakedness, or peril, or sword?

Nay, in all these things we are more than conquerors through Him that loved us. For I am persuaded, That neither death nor life, nor angels, nor principalities, nor powers, nor things present, nor things to come.

Nor height, nor depth, nor any other creature shall be able to separate us from the love of God which is in Christ Jesus.

We all have within ourselves the Christ Idea. Jesus represents God's idea of man in expression. Christ is the idea of God in man. So Jesus Christ is the perfect idea and the expression. He is the perfect man demonstrated. Jesus is the name that represents an individual expression of the Christ idea. Christ is the only begotten Son of God, or the one complete idea of perfect man in Divine Mind. We are all individualized expressions of this one idea of perfect man. Individual means "undivided."

How can we possibly be separated from God when we are the place where God shines through as us? But we say, "How about the time I was ill, or had all this terrible trouble? Certainly God seemed to be turning His back on me then."

We can look at times like this and say with Joseph, *But God meant it for good.* Joseph's brothers had sold him into slavery. He spent months in prison. Finally, he became the ruler of Egypt. When his brothers came to him for food, because there was famine in the land, they were upset when they found that the ruler of Egypt was their brother, Joseph. However, Joseph said to them, *Ye meant it for evil, but God meant it for good.* Genesis 50:20

How can we possibly know the larger plan? All things work together for good to those who love good, God. It is not too late right now to start loving everything that has ever happened to us.

We read in the scriptures:

*I will restore to you the years that the locust hath
eaten . . . and ye shall know that I am the Lord
your God, and there is none else.*   Joel 2:25, 27

If we look back and see what we call "wasted years,"
then there is something to be done. These years must
be restored. Restored means to be made beautiful
again. If we restore a painting or a house, we bring it
back to its original beauty. We need to have our years
restored so that they can be brought back to their
original beauty.

*Ezekiel said, I will overturn, and overturn, and
overturn . . . until He comes whose right it is.*
                                    Ezekiel 21:27

Our story is chapter after chapter of living. We go
through many experiences before we come to our rightful place. We would not be the person we are; we
would not have the love, the understanding, would
not be ready for whatever God has for us today, if we
had not had the experiences that we have labeled
"wasted."

Our past has been a process of unfoldment. We unfold physically and mentally from children to adults.
So too, do we unfold in spiritual consciousness. While
we have been unfolding and growing through experiences, God has been unfolding in us, loving us, mov-
ing through us, sustaining us. As He is in us right now,

so He was in us in the past. He was with us when we were having the experiences that we felt were wasted. He was there, bringing us good. He was there, helping us grow. He was there, leading us to fulfillment. He was there. How could the past have been wasted? He was there. How could we have failed? He was there. All is well. All we need to do is to restore in our own mind the Truth that God has always been with us.

The raised-up Christ consciousness is always within us, waiting only to be recognized. And by this (law of) recognition, we are blessed in all we do and think, feel and say.

Lo, I am with you always, even unto the end of the world.   Mark 28:20

3

The Second Initiation

The Baptism
Unification . . . "I AM"

The first initiation is chiefly concerned with the conquering of the idea of "separateness," and can truly be spoken of as a "Birth" in the "Manger" of our heart. The "Birth" is the awareness of the Christ within us. Now God is personal to us, God immanent, God indwelling. God is now our loving Father whose pleasure it is to "give us the Kingdom." After the "Birth" we are never again alone for we know with a certainty "God is with me."

The second initiation on the path is the Baptism. When we say Baptism, we do not necessarily mean a physical Baptism, where the candidate is either sprinkled or immersed and where he or she makes certain promises to the one who baptizes him or her. In Luke 3:3, we read of the *"Baptism of repentance unto remission of sins."* The word repentance has been interpreted to mean an admission to God of sorrow for past sin and a resolve to be good in the future.

The word translated throughout the New Testament as "repentance" is the Greek "meta-noia", which means "change of mind." The Greek particle "meta" is found in several words of comparatively ordinary usage such as metaphor, metamorphosis, metaphysics. The particle "meta" indicates transference, or transformation, or beyondness. For instance, metaphysics refers to the study of what is beyond purely observable physical science. "Noia" is from the Greek word "nous" which means "mind." The word "metanoia," therefore, has to do with transformation of the mind. It refers to a "new mind"—a new way of thinking. When Jesus said to *turn the other cheek*, He meant to change one's thought when faced by discord of any kind, to turn our attention from the human to the Divine.

The mission of John the Baptist was to bring about a change of mind. So the water baptism given Jesus by John the Baptist symbolizes a cleansing process, the letting go of all negative thoughts, resentments, bitterness, and all other attitudes that say, "God is absent." This "letting go" is the Word in the form of denial.

If we have done any piece of work incorrectly, the very first step toward getting it right is to undo (erase) the wrong and begin again from that point. Denials have an erasive or dissolving tendency. "There is no absence of Good, God, in my life" is an example of a denial, followed by a firm affirmation, "For God is all in all."

The water baptism is a cleansing, purifying process, preparing the individual to see spiritually and to discern spiritually. Baptism means to immerse in an element (any element) to a complete saturation; one can be immersed in a transformed mind as well as in water. Whenever there is a complete cleansing of the consciousness (water baptism symbology) a spiritual illumination follows. In Matthew 3:16 we read:

And Jesus, when He was baptized, went up straightway out of the water; and lo, the heavens were opened unto Him, and He saw the spirit of God descending like a dove, and lighting upon Him; and a voice from heaven, saying, "This is my beloved son, in whom I am well pleased."

The outpouring (or inpouring) of the Holy Spirit is the second baptism, the baptism of fire spoken of in Luke 3:16:

John answered, saying unto them all, "I indeed baptize you with water; but one mightier than I

cometh, the latchet of whose shoes I am not wor-
thy to unloose; he shall baptize you with the Holy
Spirit and with fire.''

This Baptism of the Holy Spirit is known as "regen-eration." Spiritual Baptism (the second baptism) has power; it is affirmative and positive. Christ represents this phase of baptism. It is the most precious gift of God and comes to those who steadfastly seek first the kingdom of God and His Righteousness.

When the disciples of Jesus wanted to restrain some-one from doing works in His Name, Jesus said, *Forbid him not* (Mark 9:39). So everyone who goes ahead and does the very best that he knows, in the Name of the Most High God (the highest good), will by virtue of his works draw upon himself the creative activity of God, the Holy Spirit.

It is interesting to note that some thirty years elapsed between the Birth (the first initiation) of Jesus and His Baptism (the second initiation), but the re-maining steps of initiation to the Resurrection were completed in three years. Apparently, once the second initiation is taken, the progress is rapid.

The second initiation deals largely with the purify-ing and developing of the mental powers and faculties and has to do with the controlling and purifying of the intellect and emotions. Just as the person who is entering the first initiation should say, "In these circumstances what would The Christ have done? Let me do the same," so the person who is entering the second initiation will watch his every thought, his every word, and say, "What would The Christ think, or say, in this circumstance? Let me think, or say, the same."

Now here is a point of which everyone who is on the path should be aware. The Christ Baptism gives us a very decided mind expansion and infuses into our thoughts and words a power that we did not possess before. The Bible says of Jesus after the baptism that *His Word was with authority*. (Mark 1:22).

When we have resolved to live in the Spirit, we have made a covenant with the Most High. We have entered into an agreement with our invisible Self that is far more binding than any man-made contract could possibly be. If we are negative, ungrateful, fearful, all of this is amplified by the very power we ourselves have given our words.

And the most powerful word is the name-nature of God.

And Moses said unto God, "Behold, when I come unto the children of Israel, and shall say unto them, the God of our fathers hath sent me unto you; and they shall say to me, 'What is His name?' What shall I say unto them?"

And God said unto Moses, "I AM THAT I AM."
Thus shalt thou say unto the children of Israel, "I
AM" hath sent me unto you:

This is My name forever, and this is My memorial
unto all generations.   Exodus 3:13, 14, 15.

Throughout the Bible we find this declaration, that
the name-nature of God is "I AM." When we say, "I
AM," we are using the great creative power of the
universe at our particular point in the universe. We
unify consciously with our God Presence by using the
name of God, "I AM."

"I AM," is the name-nature of God within us. We
are the only creature on earth that can announce, "I
AM," and herein lies the confirmation that we are
made in the image and likeness of God.

This then is our third discipline: To follow the
power words, "I AM," with words of Truth, Life,
Love, Intelligence; to refrain from using the name of
the Lord our God, our "I AM," in vain. We profane a
thing, in this case, the Name, when we put it to an im-
proper use; we violate or desecrate its true nature.

Thou shalt not take the name of the Lord thy God
in vain; for the Lord will not hold him guiltless
that taketh His Name in vain.   Exodus 20:7.

In Mathew 12:33 we read:

Therefore I say unto you, every sin and blasphemy shall be forgiven unto men; but the blasphemy against the Spirit shall not be forgiven.

The "Unforgiveable Sin" is our denial of the presence of God within us or anyone else. To do so is a declaration that our good is absent in our life. When we think of ourselves as sick, poor, miserable, we are repudiating our true nature, our "I AM."

The words "I AM" set up a strong vibration when used either in thought or the spoken word. Whatever we claim for ourselves (center our attention on) following the announcement "I AM," will tend to externalize in our body and in the body of our affairs. When we say, "I AM," we are declaring the law of our life. If we say, "I AM tired, sick, poor, fed up, disappointed, getting old," we are declaring the law for future limitation.

When we say, *"I AM Divine Life, I AM Divine Truth, I AM Divine Freedom,"* we are drawing a check on the bank of heaven, and that check will be honored with health and plenty. We know that the word of God is a conscious act and that the law of God is a mechanical reaction.

The danger point at the second stage of development is indicated in the Gospel Story by the temptation in the wilderness which followed the Baptism of Jesus.

Immediately after His Baptism, Jesus *was led up of the Spirit into the wilderness to be tempted of the devil.* (Matthew 4:1). The attainment of a higher consciousness is generally followed by what seems to be a testing period.

While Jesus was in the wilderness, fasting (abstaining from negative, destructive thoughts) and praying (communing with God), the devil (the lower nature or sense consciousness) tempted Jesus to use His powers for selfish purposes and for material gain.

The story of the wilderness temptation is told in St. Luke 4:3–14 and Matthew 4:1–11:

Then was Jesus led up of the Spirit into the wilderness to be tempted of the devil . . . and when he had fasted forty days and forty nights, he was hungered. And when the tempter came to him, he said, "If thou be the son of God, command that these stones be made bread . . ." But He answered and said, "It is written, man shall not live by bread alone, but by every word that proceedeth out of the mouth of God". . . . Then the devil taketh Him up into the Holy City and setteth Him on a pinnacle of the temple. . . and saith unto Him, "If thou be the son of God cast thyself down; for it is written, he shall give his angels charge concerning Thee: and in their hands they shall bear thee up, lest at any time thou dash thy foot against a stone".

Jesus said unto him, "It is written again, thou shalt not tempt the Lord Thy God". . . Again the devil taketh him up into an exceeding high mountain, and showeth him all the kingdoms of the world, and the glory of them; and saith unto Him, "All these things will I give Thee, if Thou wilt fall down and worship me". . . Then saith Jesus unto Him, "Get thee hence, Satan; for it is written, thou shalt worship the Lord Thy God, and Him only shalt thou serve. . . Then the devil leaveth Him and behold, angels came and ministered unto Him.

The devil first tempted Jesus, saying—*"If Thou be the Son of God, command these stones be made bread."* Jesus answered him, saying *"Man shall not live by bread alone, but by every word of God."*

Then Jesus was tempted to cast Himself down from a pinnacle of the temple to astound the populace. But Jesus said, *"It is written, thou shalt not tempt the Lord Thy God."*

Lastly, Jesus was shown all the kingdoms of the world and the glory of them, and the devil said, *"All these things will I give thee, if Thou wilt fall down and worship me."* Matthew 4:9

Jesus was tempted, even as we are, to use His powers to gratify His own ambition. However, Jesus said:

> *Get thee hence, Satan; for it is written, "Thou shalt worship the Lord Thy God, and Him only shalt thou serve."*   Matthew 4:10

At this stage, we must guard against all pride—material, intellectual, and spiritual.

At the conclusion of His forty-day fast, Jesus began His ministry, and began gathering His disciples. The disciples of Jesus represent the faculties of the mind. When the conscious mind recognizes the Christ Mind, the various faculties gradually awaken. We read in the Bible that Jesus "called His disciples to Him." The scattered faculties are drawn together and are brought to a recognition of the Master—"I AM."

We are not bound to old conditions, not for a single minute. Christ lives in us and is active in us now to help us ascend into His Consciousness of Life. The Christ in us knows that there are no hopeless situations, no incurable afflictions, no insurmountable barriers, for we are Children of God, and heirs to all the overcoming power that Jesus Christ demonstated. Ours is the power to overcome through the Christ Spirit that dwells in us, through our own "I AM."

"I AM" should be a secret, sacred prayer. Every time we feel the word "I" inside of us, we are acknowledging that God is closer than breathing and nearer than hands or feet. That "I" is the God-power, the Christ, the Spirit of God in man.

We should feel this mighty "I AM" presence baptizing every cell of our body, every atom of our Being, every emotion, every word, every thought, every act with its cleansing, healing power.

Behold "I Am" The Lord, that is My name.
Isaiah 42:8

4

The Third Initiation

The Transfiguration. . .
The Atonement. . .
Realization

The first initiation, the Birth, has to do with right conduct. The second initiation, the Baptism, has to do with right thinking.

The Transfiguration is the representation of the third initiation, expansion of consciousness. This passage opens with the phrase "After six days." After six days means it was on the seventh day. Seven is the number of completion. It is the number that leads us to Christ illumination.

And after six days, Jesus taketh Peter, James and John his Brother—and bringeth them up into a high mountain apart.

And was transfigured before them: and His face did shine as the sun, and his raiment was white as the light.

And, behold, there appeared unto them, Moses and Elijah talking with Him.

Then answered Peter, and said unto Jesus, "Lord, it is good for us to be here; if thou wilt, let us make here three tabernacles; one for thee, and one for Moses, and one for Elias."

While he yet spake, behold, a bright cloud over-shadowed them: and behold a voice out of the cloud, which said, "This is my beloved Son, in whom I am well pleased: Hear ye Him!"

And when the disciples heard it, they fell on their face, and were sore afraid. And Jesus came and touched them, and said, "Arise and be not afraid."

And when they had lifted up their eyes, they saw no man, save Jesus only.

And as they came down from the mountain Jesus charged them, saying, "Tell the vision to no man, until the Son of man be risen again from the dead."   Matthew 17:1-9

Jesus went to the mountain, a high state of con-sciousness, to pray. He took with Him Peter, James, and John. These three disciples are three of the twelve aspects of our own character, our own nature, which must be "disciplined." Peter stands for the thinking state in man that was raised up to Faith. James was the disciple of Wisdom, and John, the disciple of Love. These, then, are the three aspects with which we rise to a high consciousness in prayer and meditation: Faith, Wisdom and Love.

The disciples of Jesus represent the faculties of the mind. After one has been illumined by Truth, the scattered faculties are drawn together and are brought to a recognition of the Master—"I AM."

This gathering together of our powers is an orderly process, and we will find that it proceeds right along the lines laid down in Jesus' choosing of His disciples as recorded in the gospels. Charles Fillmore explains, in *The Twelve Powers of Man*, what each of the disciples represents. The first disciple that Jesus called was PETER.

PETER represents Faith in things spiritual, faith in God. We begin our religious experience by having faith in God as omnipresent, all-wise, all-loving, all-powerful. When Jesus said to His disciples, *But who say ye that I Am?* Only (Simon) Peter answered:

Thou are the Christ, the Son of the Living God.

And Jesus answered, *Thou art Peter, and upon this rock (Faith) I will build My church, and the gates of Hades shall not prevail against it. I will give unto thee the keys of the kingdom of heaven.* Matthew 16:18, 19

It was not only to the personal PETER that Jesus gave the keys to His Kingdom, but to all who through Faith apply the Truth of Being.

ANDREW, the strength faculty, is the next disciple to be called or brought into manifestation. We grow weak under material thoughts and burdens. Jesus said, *Come unto me, all ye that labour and are heavy laden, and I will give you rest.* (Matthew 11:28) We must remember that:

He performeth that which is given me to do.
                                                    Job 23:14

JAMES, the son of Zebedee, represents discrimination and good judgment in dealing with substantial things. JAMES is the faculty in us that chooses and determines. It may be in the matter of food, or human relationships, or career choice or anything else where discrimination and good judgment are needed. The spiritual side of the JAMES faculty is intuition, quick-knowing.

JOHN represents the love faculty. There are times, especially under great stress, when we long for the simple assurance of God's love. We need to know in our heart that "God loves me." The world may seem to be against me but God loves me. Christ is the revelation of the Love of God. Jesus the Christ was the first to reveal to men the true nature of God, God as Love.

When Jesus called the disciples: PETER, JAMES, and JOHN, there was in His consciousness a quickening of Faith, Wisdom and Love. These three disciples are mentioned more often than His other disciples because they are most essential in the expression of a well-balanced person. ANDREW (strength) was also among the first because he represents the stability that lies at the foundation of every true character.

PHILLIP represents power—more especially the power of the word. BARTHOLOMEW represents the imagination. We should not imagine anything but good, because under the law of thought our imagining will sooner or later come into expression.

Man has faculties of elimination, of cleansing, as well as of appropriation. The Renunciation disciple is THADDEUS, also known as JUDE. THOMAS represents the understanding power of man. He is called the doubter because he wants to know everything.

MATTHEW is the disciple of the will. JAMES, the son of Alphaeus, represents the Divine Order. SIMON THE CANAANITE, represents zeal. JUDAS, who betrayed Jesus, governs the life consciousness of the body. JUDAS is selfish; greed is his "devil." But JUDAS can be redeemed. JUDAS generates the life of the body. We need life, but life must be guided in Divine ways.

The ancients believed that the twelve powers of man had twelve corresponding centers in the body. According to them, the Christ, the "I AM," has His throne in the top of the head. This is the mountain where Jesus so often went to pray. The love center (JOHN) is in the heart; the strength center (ANDREW) is in the small of the back; the imagination center (BARTHOLOMEW) between the eyes; the power center (PHILLIP) at the root of the tongue, "from where the word is spoken."

The faith center (PETER) is the pineal gland. The understanding center (THOMAS) is in the front brain; his collaborator MATTHEW, the will, occupies the same brain area. The zeal center (SIMON, THE CANNANAEN) is at the medulla, the base of the brain; the wisdom center (JAMES, SON OF ZEBEDEE) is the solar plexus, or sun center; the center of order (JAMES, SON OF ALPHAEUS) is at the navel; the renunciation, or elimination center (THADDAEUS) in the abdominal region and the life conserver center (JUDAS) is in the generative organs.

At the Transfiguration, Jesus went up into the mountain to pray—this means an elevation of thought and aspiration from the mortal to the spiritual viewpoint. The Transfiguration is always preceded by a change of mind, metanoia. In the Transfiguration we are lifted from the material to the spiritual.

The story of the Transfiguration is that Jesus the Christ took the three disciples who were nearest to Him in thought, Peter (Faith), James (Wisdom), and John (Love) up to Mount Tabor and then was transfigured before them. When the mind is exalted in prayer, one is indeed transfigured. The scriptures relate that *His face did shine as the sun, and His raiment was white as light.*

The story tells also that at the Transfiguration there appeared Moses (the law giver), and Elijah (one of the greatest of the Jewish Prophets). Moses and Elijah were the chief figures of the old dispensation. The two dispensations, or methods of approach to Truth, are that of the following of the law, represented by Moses and Elijah as the law-givers; and of Jesus who was about to establish a new dispensation, the Christ Principle. So obedience to the truths given by the law and the prophets is the process by which we rise to the Christ Consciousness.

The Transfiguration is a constant realization of our unity with God. This is our atonement, our at-one-ment. Our day of selfishness is over and our day of selflessness has come. This day delivers us from all our burdens. We say with Jesus:

All things have been delivered unto me of My Father (Matthew 11:27).

We do not breathe for ourselves, but rather God breathes in us and as us. We do not have lives of our own, but we feel the life of God surging through our bodies. We do not think and speak by ourselves alone; we think and speak God's thoughts after Him. Neither do we have possessions of our own, nor cares, nor troubles about our lives or our families; we leave all these things to God.

Jesus was the great wayshower to the attainment of this realization of Spirit. When we see the parallel between our experiences and the Transfiguration of Jesus, we gain confidence to go forward.

At the Transfiguration, Jesus was lifted up by Peter, James, and John (Faith, Wisdom, and Love). Whenever we dwell on these virtues and try to live up to them, they are exalted in consciousness, and they go up with us to the Mount of Transfiguration. We may think that the uplifting was just a passing exaltation, but it stamps itself on our soul and body.

Jesus, on the Mount of Transfiguration, spoke of His death that was to follow. This death was of material sense in order to be born of the Spirit. At the Transfiguration, the disciple must be free from the possibility of being enslaved by external things—by the world of form. At this stage, we are "stewards" only, never "owners." We may have great wealth; it is no longer ours. We may have mental ability; it is no longer ours. We must use it only for service.

We must never worship effect. Never hate, fear, or love effect. That is where idolatry comes in—the worship of form. The very moment that a form becomes a necessity in our experience, we are placing our dependence, our happiness on a form instead of the invisible which is the cause of the form.

Spiritual supply is ever present; this we cannot lose. If we have this realization, we can never be separated from any form of supply. Realization is demonstration. It is the realization of God's presence that makes the demonstration. Demonstration is the result of realization.

We say that God is everywhere. This is true. However, God is only manifest where God is realized. If we cannot realize, feel the actual presence of God, then insofar as we are concerned, God is not there. God is everywhere in the absolute spiritual sense, but God is not everywhere as far as we are concerned unless we are conscious of the presence of God. If we are conscious of the presence of God, of the activity of God in everything, then it is so to us.

Neither shall they say, "Lo here!" or "Lo there," for the Kingdom of God is within you. Luke 17:21

Wherever we are is a Holy Place because we have our individual portable shrine, our Holy of Holies, within us. Everyone and everything we encounter, everything we do, is blessed by the certain knowledge of our Holy Christ Self, and the ground whereon we stand is indeed "Holy Ground."

The Transfiguration lies before everyone of us. We are here and now divine; the Spirit in us is a spark of the Divine Spirit. We need only to let it show forth in every act, every thought, and every word. We need only to lift up our thoughts and behold the Spiritual Reality of every form.

This is to *Know the truth that sets us free* (John 8:32).

TWELVES POWERS OF MAN

Attribute	Disciple	Nerve Centers	The Natural Man	Lifted up Faculties
Faith	Peter	Center of Brain	Intellec-tual faith	Rooted in love
Strength	Andrew	Small of back	Physical strength	God is my strength
Discrimi-nation	James, son of Zebedee	Pit of stomach	Human judgment	Divine guidance
Love	John	Back of the heart	Eros love	Agape love
Power	Phillip	Root of tongue	Persuasion, criticism	I am the power of God in action! Praise and glorify

Imagination	Bartholomew	Between the eyes	Worry that God is absent	See the good and praise it!
Understanding	Thomas	Front Brain	Intellect	Intuition Instant knowing
Will	Matthew	Center front brain	Human will Ego	God's will as my will
Order	James, son of Alphaeus	Navel	Chance	The Divine plan according to principle
Zeal	Simon	Back of head	Excitement	Enthusiasm
Renunciation	Thaddeus	Abdominal region	Martyrdom	Release the past Let go and let God!
Life	Judas	Generative function	Sensuality	Creativity

5

The Fourth Initiation
The Celebration . . . *Thanksgiving*

The events attributed to Holy Week and the Crucifixion symbolize the fourth state of a Neophyte's spiritual unfoldment. The Fourth initiation differs from all the others, in that it has a strange double aspect of suffering and victory. Each of the earlier Initiations in our Christian Religion was symbolized by one definite fact: The Birth, the Baptism, the Transfiguration. But in order to present this Fourth Initiation, a series of events seems necessary. This last week, Holy Week, is really a recapitulation of the other Initiations.

The first stage of this Fourth Initiation is the celebration known as Palm Sunday, as told in Matthew 21:1–11 and John 12:12–19

And when they drew nigh unto Jerusalem, and were come to Bethany, unto the Mount of Olives, then sent Jesus two disciples, saying unto them,

*"go into the village over against you, and straight-
way ye shall find an ass tied, and a colt with her:
loose them, and bring them unto me. And if any
man say ought unto you, ye shall say, 'The Lord
hath need of them'; and straightway he will send
them."*

*All this was done, that it might be fulfilled which
was spoken by the prophet, saying, tell ye the
daughter of Sion, "Behold, Thy King cometh unto
thee, meek, and sitting upon an ass, and a colt the
foal of an ass."*

*And the disciples went, and did as Jesus com-
manded them, and brought the ass, and the colt,
and put on them their clothes and they set him
thereon.*

*And a very great multitude spread their garments
in the way; others cut down branches from the
trees, and strawed them in the way. And the mul-
titudes that went before, and that followed, cried,
saying, "Hosanna to the son of David: blessed is
he that cometh in the name of the Lord; Hosanna
in the highest."*

*And when He was come into Jerusalem, all the
city was moved, saying "Who is this?" And the
multitude said, "This is Jesus the prophet of Nazareth of Galilee."*

In Oriental countries, in Biblical times, kings and rulers rode the ass. The characteristics of the ass are meekness, stubborness, persistency, and endurance. To ride these is to make them obedient to one's will. Jesus portrayed the mastery of the animal nature by riding the ass into Jerusalem. So long as the animal rules, the man is a slave. When the I AM man, represented by Jesus, takes charge, the vitality is no longer wasted but is directed, is ridden. Jesus said, *The Lord hath need of them*, meaning that these forces of the so-called lower nature in man are necessary to his full expression. A man or woman with the animal nature asleep or suppressed is but partially alive. The vital fires are in this part of his being; but they must be disciplined, i.e. "ridden."

Jesus enjoyed this one earthly triumph, largely as a result of raising Lazarus from the dead.

It has been said that the Prayer of Thanksgiving is the prayer of appropriation. This is the manner in which Jesus prayed when he raised Lazarus from the tomb.

"Father, I thank the that thou hast heard me, and I know thou hearest me always."

And when he had thus spoke, he cried with a loud voice, "Lazarus, come forth". And he that was dead came forth.   John 11: 41–44

The raising of Lazarus from the dead signifies the restoring to consciousness of the idea of youth, which is asleep in the subjective (subconsciousness) or the tomb of the body. People grow old because they let the youth idea fall asleep. This idea is not dead, but is sleeping, and the understanding I AM (Jesus the Christ) goes to awaken it.

This awakening of youthful energies is necessary to those on the path. Eternal youth is one of those God-given ideas that man loves. The scripture records tell us that when Jesus was told of the death of Lazarus, He wept. (John 11:35 & 36)

Jesus wept.

Then said the Jews, "Behold how He loved him!"

On Monday and Tuesday of Holy Week, Jesus spent much time teaching the people. In fact, nearly half of His recorded sayings are said to have been delivered on those two days. This is symbolic of what really takes place. At this stage, the Disciple attracts some attention, and gains a certain amount of popularity and recognition. He (she) takes advantage of this popularity to teach.

After Jesus' triumphal entry into Jerusalem, He drove the money changers from the temple, as recorded in Matthew 21:12, 13. The money changers represent dishonest thoughts of materiality and greed. The consciousness must be cleansed of these thoughts if the body temple is to be kept pure and holy. We must cast out all such destructive thoughts and attitudes.

On Wednesday, Jesus and His Disciples apparently remained in Bethany, preparing for the Passover Supper. Let us briefly examine the story of the Passover as told in the Book of Exodus and see the similarity to our Easter Story. Just as the Paschal Lamb Sacrifice, for the Jews, commemorated their redemption from bondage in Egypt, so the sacrifice of Jesus, for the Christians, was considered their redemption from the bondage of mortality and sin.

The Passover is a "passing over," or out of, one state of consciousness into another. It celebrates the deliverance of a people from Egypt, materiality. In the Easter Story, it is the deliverance of man from death.

The various plagues brought upon the Egyptians (materiality) by the Lord (Law) through Moses (the drawing-out process) is symbolic of what happens when the presiding intelligence (Pharaoh) opposes the higher life. The "first-born" of the Egyptians is the highest concept of life that the physical man possesses. When the Divine Word or "Angel of the Lord" passes through consciousness, a transformation takes place in his thought. If the consciousness is in materiality (Egypt) this "first-born" concept is destroyed. If the mind is set on higher things (Jews, Divine ideas), then this "first-born" is saved from destruction.

The putting of the blood of the lamb on the two side posts and the lintel of the door of the house typifies the elevating of our life to the open door of our mind.

So long as there is a hidden, secret use of God's life in our habits and ways that we are not willing that all should know, just so long will the the bondage of Egypt's Pharoah hold us in its clutches. The whole man must be pure, and his inner life must be made so open and free that we will not be afraid to blazon it upon the very doors of our house, where all who pass may read.

Then the scriptures say that the Lord will execute His judgment and those who have purified the life of the lamb (the body) will escape the messenger (thought) of death.

The spiritual man, the true ego "I AM," is the only rightful heir to the Divine Inheritance, Spiritual Consciousness. We, as individuals, must awaken from the dream of mortality, leave Egypt (flesh consciousness) forever, and cross the Red Sea (the boundary line where we sacrifice every tie that binds us to the past), go through the wilderness, through the waters of Jordan and plant our feet (understanding) on Canaan's land, our Divine Inheritance.

Wednesday of Holy Week was the day of preparation for the Passover Supper and it was also the day that Judas Iscariot made plans to betray Jesus. Matthew 26:14-16; Mark 14:10, 11; Luke 22:3-6

What motive prompted Judas to bargain with the Jews to betray Jesus? Perhaps Judas felt that Jesus' cause was now lost and that he should salvage what he could from the three years of following Him. Or perhaps Judas thought that the betrayal would bring matters to a climax and and force Jesus to declare Himself to be the Messiah and invoke the wrath of God upon His persecutors. Whatever the motive, Judas went to Jerusalem on Wednesday night, and asked the Jewish authorities what they would pay him to deliver Jesus to them. They offered him thirty pieces of silver and Judas agreed.

Judas represents life. However, in Judas Iscariot we find the unredeemed life forces that, unless handled spiritually, betray the Christ or Spiritual Life. Judas is typical of that which exists in humanity, which even though it has caught the higher vision of life, The

Christ, still resorts to underhanded methods. When we are tempted to succumb to sense desires of an unworthy nature, it means that Judas in in control.

Judas also symbolizes desire, appropriation, acquisitiveness. Acquisitiveness is a legitimate faculty of the mind, but covetousness is its Judas. This is the Judas in ourselves—convetousness, greed.

The first step in redeeming our Judas faculty is to affirm our unity with God. Love overcomes all selfishness, and transforms the sense man into the Spiritual Man.

The next day, Thursday, was the day of the Passover Supper. The story is told in Matthew 26:26–30; Luke 22:19, and St. John 13:2–17:

And as they were eating, Jesus took bread, and blessed it, and broke it, and gave it to the disciples, and said, "Take, eat: This is My body."

And He took the cup, and gave thanks, and gave it to them, saying "Drink ye all of it."

For this is my blood of the New Testament, which is shed for the remission of sins.

Matthew 26:26–28.

Upon this passage the Eucharist, the Sacrament of the Lord's Supper, was founded. It commemorates the Last Supper of Jesus with His Disciples. The "upper chamber'' where the Last Supper took place is our high state of mind when our thoughts are turned to Spiritual things. It may be obtained through prayer, or in Spiritual Meditation.

In the ritual of the Holy Eucharist the Rhythm of Creation is followed. All great rituals are based on the one primordial ritual, the descent of God into matter. The descent of the Divine Life takes place in the consecration of the bread and wine. In rituals, such as the Eurcharist, we not only benefit from the psychological effect of the actions, but we also take part in the reality of things we cannot understand. The great lesson of all ritual is that our entire life should become a ritual, that is to say, controlled, aware action, directing force exactly where and as it is needed.

Metaphysically, the Lord's Supper is God's covenant with mankind through His perfect idea, Christ Jesus. The bread symbolizes the Spiritual Substance of the body. The wine symbolizes the Blood of Jesus Christ, or Spiritual Life.

We eat the body of Jesus Christ mentally, by affirming the one Spiritual substance to be the substance of our body, and we drink His blood by affirming and realizing our oneness with the one divine, omnipresent Life of Spirit. Wine symbolizes the vitality that forms the connecting link betweeen the soul and body. The breaking of bread (universal substance) is the stirring into action, in consciousness, of the inner substance of Spirit.

We live by continually drawing from the Infinite Spirit. We do this automatically, but we also have the power to consciously use the Universal Energy for any specific purpose that we will. This combination of dependence and control is perfectly symbolized by the acts of eating and drinking. We cannot do without food, but it is at our own discretion to select what and when we shall eat. And eating is a very personal matter, as is our spiritual advancement; no one else can do it for us.

So it is in Spiritual Communion; we realize the Christ Principle (the perfect pattern) in our lives by consciously partaking of the bread (Substance) and the wine (Spirit) in remembrance of Him (The Christ Principle).

To "eat" the Body of Christ is to make words of praise and strength and thanksgiving ours by thinking on them, "eating" them until they are part of us. The Christ is the Word of God, the Logos. So to "eat" the Body of Christ is to make Spiritual Words our own by Being the Word.

And the Word was made flesh and dwelt among us!   John 1:14

We read in St. Matthew 26:27, *And He took the cup, and gave thanks.*

The "cup" is the consciousness of eternal life which Jesus shared with His Disciples and with us.

An idea dominant in the time of Judaism and of Paganism was that by the eating of sacrificed and dedicated food, a union was consummated between the worshipper and his deity. In other words, through this "eating," the worshipper took on the attributes of deity.

In John 13:21–35, we find that before the Disciples were finished eating, Judas left the room. Since Judas was the keeper of their common funds, the Disciples did not think too much of his early departure, possibly thinking he had gone to settle accounts for the dinner.

However, Jesus knew that Judas would betray Him, but He made no effort to stop this act of betrayal. Sense-consciousness (Judas) betrays us every day, yet it would be unwise to destroy it before its time because at its foundation it is good.

Throughout the Gospels it is made clear that Jesus was acting deliberately and that He chose His Disciples, Judas, as well as the rest, for the part that they had to play in this drama which was foreseen and arranged in every detail.

We are told in the Gospels, John 13:2–5; 12–17, that when Jesus and His Disciples had finished eating, He rose from the table and girded Himself with a towel, then poured water into a basin and commenced to wash His Disciples' feet. To wash the feet seems a menial thing, but in this humble way Jesus taught and exemplified the willingness of Divine Love to serve.

Jesus signifies the I AM and the feet represent that phase of the understanding which connects one with the outer or manifest world and reveals the right relationship toward worldly conditions in general. The washing of the Disciples' feet by Jesus, therefore, typifies not only a willingness to serve, but a cleansing process or a denial of personality and materiality.

The highest service to God is to serve Him in the person of our fellowmen. All religions teach much the same Truths, but the main theme in Christianity is to develop ourselves by means of service to others, realizing the truth of the words which Jesus said:

Inasmuch as ye have done it unto the least of these
My little ones, ye have done it unto Me.
                                        Matthew 25:40

This is the "bread cast upon the waters"! It is only that which we give out that can come back to us. There is nothing out in the world that has any way of coming to us except what we have placed out in the world. There is no question about this principle. Life is a completeness in us, and as we permit it to flow out, it flows back. "The bread on the water" that comes to us is the bread we place there. If we draw in another's loaf of bread, we will find that in some way or other, our fingers will be burned. We have a right only to the Bread of Life that we place on the waters of life.

One of the secrets of the Bible is "What have you in the house?" Use that. Start the flow.

We are told in II King 4th Chapter of a widow who came to Elisha concerning her money problems. The creditors were going to take her two sons to be bond-men in payment of a debt.

And Elisha said unto her, "Tell me, what hast thou in the house?" And she said, "Thine handmaid hath not anything in the house, save a pot of oil."

Then he said, "Go, borrow thee vessels abroad of all thy neighbors, even empty vessels; borrow not a few.

And when thou art come in, thou shalt shut the door upon thee and upon thy sons, and shalt pour out into all those vessels."

And it came to pass, when the vessels were full, that she said unto her son, "Bring me yet a vessel". And he said unto her, "There is not a vessel more." And the oil stayed.

Then she came and told the man of God. And He said, "Go sell the oil, and pay thy debt, and live thou and thy children of the rest."

This passage is rich in instruction. The widow prepared to receive by securing the empty vessels; she "shut the door," did not talk about what she was doing, and then she started to pour. From the fullness of what she had "in the house," she started the flow. She primed the pump. If it is money we seem to have need of, we find a place to give; if it is love, we find someone (or something) to love. If we have a need for health, then start to demonstrate health by using the energy and praising the health that is manifest. Whatever we give returns in kind. The Bible states very clearly the Law of Circulation.

Give, and it shall be given unto you: Good measure, pressed down, shaken together, and running over.   Luke 6:38

It is not only more blessed to give than to receive, it is also more productive—for what we receive is not multiplied; what we give is multiplied! Receiving is merely giving on its return trip. Ernest Holmes states in the SCIENCE OF MIND: "When the law of circulation is retarded, a stagnation results. It is only as we allow the divine current to flow through us and out, that we really express life. The law of giving and receiving is definite."

The River Jordan is an unusual river because it has no outlet to the sea. It simply dies in the barren desert of Southern Judea, in the Dead Sea. The Dead Sea has no outlet—it cannot give!

In truth, we do not need anything, we *are* everything, but we must *Let It Flow!* So giving is our demonstration, not receiving. We demonstrate health by using the energy and praising the health that is manifest; we demonstrate abundance by giving of what we have. We demonstrate by using what we have in "full faith, believing." And then, that which we have demonstrated by giving, is returned to us.

> *Good measure, pressed down, shaken together, and running over!*   Luke 6:38

Before they left the upper room, Jesus told Peter that he would deny Him *Thrice before the cock crows.* But Peter said, *Though I should die with Thee, yet will I not deny Thee.* (Matthew 24:35) However, Peter did deny Jesus three times. Peter (Faith) was one of the first Disciples that Jesus called. Faith is one of the first Spiritual faculties to be called into expression by everyone who would follow Jesus in the overcoming life.

The leading characteristic of Peter (Faith) before he is firmly established in Spiritual consciousness is changeableness. He typifies that state of unsteadiness which fluctuates from the Spiritual to the material.

Peter, the wavering, denying one, is in reality Faith, a rock. When Faith works through the intellect, it is subject to all the winds and waves of sense thought; but when it is firmly rooted in love, we are told that "the gates of Hades shall not prevail against it."

The Spiritual import of Peter's repeated affirmations of love, as given in John 21:15–17, is that steadfastness of Faith is developed through love. Peter wavered in his Faith many times because he was not established in love. Until Faith is thoroughly identified with the Christ, we will find that the Peter faculty in us is a regular weather-vane. It will, in all sincerity, affirm its allegiance to Spirit, and then in the hour of adversity will deny that it ever knew Spirit. This, however, is the probationary period. When we have trained it, Faith, to look to Christ in all things, then it is indeed our "Rock."

While they were still in the upper room, Jesus spoke the comforting words recorded in the 14th Chapter of John. He knew the Disciples would have trials to meet after He had left them and He said:

Let not your heart be troubled: believe in God, believe also in Me. In My Father's house are many mansions; if it were not so, I would have told you; for I go to prepare a place for you.

Even as we believe in God, we should also believe in the Christ, God's Presence in us. When we do, human anxiety passes.

And if I go and prepare a place for you, I come again, and will receive you unto Myself, that where I am—here ye may be also!   John 14:1-3

Thomas (Understanding) protested that the Apostles knew neither where Jesus was going nor the way. Jesus answered him, saying:

"I am the Way, and the Truth, and the Life: no one cometh unto the Father, but by Me."   John 14:6

Then Phillip asked that the Disciples be shown the Father, and Jesus answered him:

Have I been so long a time with you, and dost thou not know me, Philip? He that hath seen me hath seen the Father. Believest thou not that I am in the Father, and the Father in Me? The words that I say unto you I speak not from myself: but the Father abiding in me doeth His works.

Verily, verily, I say unto you, he that believeth in me, the works that I do shall he do also; and greater works than these shall he do; because I go unto the Father. And whatsoever ye shall ask in

*My name that will I do, that the Father may be
glorified in the Son. If ye shall ask anything in My
name, that will I do.*

*If ye love me, ye will keep My commandments.
And I will pray the Father, and He shall give you
another comforter, that He may abide with you
forever, even the Spirit of Truth.*

*He that hath My commandments, and keepeth
them, he it is that loveth Me; and he that loveth
Me shall be loved of My Father, and I will love
him and will manifest Myself unto him.*

John 14:9-17 & 21

In this scripture, Jesus, representing the "I AM,"
gave assurance of Divine cooperation to those who are
loyal in thought and word to the Truth.

Jesus continued:

*Peace I leave with you; My peace I give unto you;
not as the world giveth, give I unto you. Let not
your heart be troubled, neither let it be fearful . . .
Arise, let us go hence.*   John 14:27, 31

With these words, Jesus and the Disciples left the
upper room of the Last Supper and walked down the
road toward the Garden of Gethsemane.

6

The Fourth Initiation Continues

The Garden of Gethsemane. . . Surrender . . . Thy Will Be Done!

We are following, in consciousness, the wayshower Jesus, through the Birth, the attack by Herod, the Baptism, the Temptation in the wilderness by the devil, and now the final steps on His way to the Crucifixion. The Fourth Initiation starts with Jesus' triumphal entry into Jerusalem, Palm Sunday.

Judas had left the meal early to make plans for the betrayal. Later Jesus and the other Disciples left the upper room and set out for the Garden of Gethsemane. As they walked, Jesus lifted up His eyes and prayed:

Father, the hour is come: glorify Thy Son, that Thy Son may glorify Thee: As Thou hast given him power over all flesh, that He should give eternal life to as many as Thou has given Him.

And this is Life Eternal, that they might know
Thee the only true God, and Jesus Christ, whom
Thou hast sent. I have glorified thee on earth;
I have finished the work which Thou gavest Me
to do.

And now , O Father, glorify Thou Me with Thine
own Self with the glory which I had with Thee
before the world was.   John 17:1–5

To glorify means to "magnify with praise, to en-
hance with Spiritual splendor, to adorn." Jesus was
asking for a full and complete unification of His consciousness with that of the Father. Jesus realized that
He had been given all authority over the flesh. He was
holding the realization not only for His own glorifica-
tion, but also for that of His Disciples, for all of us.

The Garden of Gethsemane was a garden near Jerusalem, at the foot of the Mount of Olives; it was the
scene of the agony and betrayal of Jesus, as told in
Matthew 26:36–44.

Metaphysically, the Garden of Gethsemane is the
struggle that takes place within the consciousness
when Truth is realized as the one reality. The suffering
that the soul undergoes in giving up its cherished
"forms" or in letting go of human consciousness is
often agony.

The work of each of us is to incorporate the Christ Mind in soul and in body. The process of eliminating the old consciousness and entering into the new may be compared to Gethsemane. The meaning of Gethsemane is "oil press." A press is an emblem of trial, distress, agony—while oil points to Spirit and illumination.

We read in Matthew:

And he took Peter and the two sons of Zebedee apart with him to pray.

The two sons of Zebedee, James and John, are Wisdom and Love; Peter represents Faith. So the faculties that are uppermost at this time are Faith, Wisdom, and Love. These same disciples were with Jesus at the time of his Transfiguration.

Then saith He unto them, "My soul is exceeding sorrowful, even unto death: tarry ye here, and watch with me."

And He went a little farther, and fell on His face, and prayed, saying, "O My Father, if it be possible, let this cup pass from Me: nevertheless not as I will, but as Thou wilt."

And He cometh unto the disciples, and findeth them asleep, and saith unto Peter, "What, could

*ye not watch with me one hour? Watch and pray
that ye enter not into temptation: the Spirit indeed
is willing, but the flesh is weak."*

*He went away again the second time, and prayed,
saying, "Oh my Father, if this cup may not pass
away from me, except I drink it, Thy will be
done."* Matthew 26:38–42

In Luke 22:44–45 we read:

*And there appeared an angel unto him from
heaven, strengthening him,*

*And being in an agony he prayed more earnestly:
and his sweat was as it were great drops of blood
falling down to the ground,*

*And when he rose up from prayer, and was come
to his disciples, He found them sleeping for sorrow.*

Jesus went away again and prayed the third time,
saying the same words. After praying the third time,
Jesus was completely at peace. Looking again on the
sleeping Disciples, He said:

*Sleep on now, and take your rest; behold, the hour
is at hand, and the Son of man is betrayed into the
hand of sinners. Arise, let us be going: behold, he
is at hand that betrayeth me.* Matthew 26:45–46

Several hours had passed since Judas left the upper room where the Last Supper was held. He had gone to the High Priest and had told them that this was the time to turn Jesus over to the Jews. The High Priest gave Judas an escort of armed men and Judas, knowing where Jesus was likely to be, led them to the Garden of Gethsemane. He gave them a sign, saying *"Whomsoever I shall kiss, that is He; take Him, and lead Him away safely."* Mark 14:44. When Judas approached Jesus, he greeted Him and kissed Him.

Defense seemed useless, especially as Jesus made no effort to save Himself, and the Disciples stood helplessly by; all but Peter. Peter drew a sword and severed the ear of Malchus, a servant of the High Priest. Instantly Jesus rebuked Peter: *"Put up thy sword."*

Then said Jesus unto him, "Put up thy sword into his place: for all they that take the sword shall perish with the sword. Thinkest thou that I cannot now pray to My Father, and He shall presently give Me more than twelve legions of angels? But how then shall the scriptures be fulfilled, that thus it must be?"   Matthew 26:52–54

Then Jesus touched the ear of Malchus and it was healed. Malchus, the High Priest's servant, symbolizes the limited understanding and judgment of the ruling power that the High Priest represents. Jesus' healing of the ear no doubt meant that we should not use our faith destructively, and that limited understanding and judgment should be healed.

The Disciples were greatly upset when they saw a multitude armed with "swords and staves." We read in Matthew 26:56, *Then all the Disciples left Him and fled.* So Jesus, left alone, was led, a captive, to the palace of the High Priest, Caiaphas. Caiaphas represents the ruling religious thought force that is entirely intellectual. He has no conception of Spirit.

Jesus was accused of the serious crime of blasphemy for saying that He was the Son of God. However, the accusers missed the point, for Jesus' teaching was that we are all the Sons of God.

Jesus answered them, "Is it not written in your Law, I said, ye are gods?"   John 10:34

Behold, what manner of love the Father has bestowed upon us, that we should be called the Sons of God: Therefore the world knoweth us not, because it knew Him not.

Beloved, now are we the Sons of God, and it doth not yet appear what we shall be: But we know that, when He shall appear, we shall be like Him: For we shall see Him as He is.

And every man that hath this hope in him puri-
fieth himself, even as He is pure.   I John 3:1–3

Jesus was given two trials: one religious and the other civil. The reason for this double legal procedure was that although the Sanhedrin could try both civil and religious cases affecting the Jews, it could not give an order for the execution of a prisoner on whom it had passed the death sentence. Only Pontius Pilate had this power.

Therefore, when the Sanhedrin condemned Jesus to death, it had to ask Pilate to issue the Order of the Crucifixion. Crucifixion was a Roman form of execution. If the Sanhedrin had been able to inflict the death penalty, Jesus would have been stoned to death, the Jewish form of execution.

Pilate granted the request that Jesus be sentenced to death, although he said, "*I find no crime in Him,*" and washed his hands to signify this.

When Jesus said to Pilate, "*To this end have I been born, and to this end am I come into the world, that I should bear witness unto the truth.*" Pilate (human will) said to Him, "*What is truth?*" John 18:38

About this time Peter had denied Jesus for the third time. Immediately a cock crowed, and Peter remembered the words which Jesus had said, "*Before the cock crows, thou shalt deny Me thrice. And Peter went out, and wept bitterly."* Matthew 26:75

Matthew 27:3–8:

Then Judas, which had betrayed Him, when he saw that He was condemned, repented himself, and brought again the thirty pieces of silver to the Chief Priests and Elders. Saying, "I have sinned in that I have betrayed innocent blood." And they said, "What is that to us?" And he cast down the pieces of silver in the temple, and departed and went and "hanged himself."

And the Chief Priests took the silver pieces, and said, "It is not lawful for to put them into the treasury, because it is the price of blood."

And they took counsel, and bought with them the potter's field, to bury strangers in. Wherefore that field was called, the field of blood, unto this day.

We read that Judas "repented himself," that he "hanged himself." The Greek word "meta-noia" that was translated in the Bible as "repentance" actually means a transformation of mind or "change of mind." And this, we are told, is all that is needed to "enter the Kingdom." Yet Judas "repented himself," and still he "hanged himself."

According to Nicoll, in *The Mark*, there are two Greek words that have been translated to mean "repentance." One is "meta-noia"; the other is equivalent to the Latin "poenitet me" meaning penitence, or sorrow for wrong doing. This is exactly from where our ordinary word "repentance" comes. Yet these Greek words of such vastly different values are translated as exactly the same word in English.

Sorrow, or penitence, may lead to "meta-noia," yet it is not "meta-noia," transformation of mind. Judas "repented unto himself." This means that Judas did not repent in the true sense of the word. He had a change of feeling; he was sorry. He did not have a "change of mind."

This type of repentance is only self-hatred, and self-hatred is suicidal. Disillusionment and disgust may be a step toward repentance, but they are not repentance. Very often people "repent unto themselves" and truly suffer; they are sorry for their lot, but are not sorry for having offended God, their own Divinity.

When we experience true repentance, transformation of mind, we turn our attention from the human, the world of form, to the Divine Perfection within us.

The death of Judas signifies the dying out of the un-redeemed life forces. In giving our attention to Christ, as Jesus did, the greedy, selfish desires are eliminated.

Matthias, who represents the lifting up of the life faculty, was later selected to replace Judas as a Disciple.

The fullest account of the appearance of the Jewish leaders and Jesus before the Roman ruler Pilate is given in John 18:38–48. The Trial, resulting in the Crucifixion, symbolizes a man (Pilate) who is controlled by human consciousness. Pilate gave the order under duress.

Pilate wanted to release Jesus and order Barabbas crucified. Barabbas was the prisoner charged with insurrection and murder, who was held at Jerusalem. However, the Jews demanded that he (Barabbas) be released instead of Jesus. Barabbas means "rebellion and hatred."

The people demanded that rebellion and hatred be released and Jesus (love) be crucified.

So Pilate handed Jesus over to the Roman guards. Having first flogged Him, the soldiers made a crown of thorny twigs and put it on His head. They clothed Him in a purple robe and pretended to worship Him. After the Roman soldiers had again mocked Jesus, they stripped Him of the purple robe, put on Him His own garments, and a cross was laid on His shoulders.

According to historians, it was customary for a criminal to carry his cross to the place of execution. However, in Matthew 27:32, we read that a man named

Simon helped Him. Simon means one who listens and obeys. It may be summed up in the word "receptivity." So, receptivity to the Christ helps us carry our cross.

> *And in Matthew 27:33, they came to a place called Golgotha, that is to say, 'A place of a skull.'*

Golgotha, also called Calvary, is a place just outside Jerusalem, a hill, where Jesus was crucified. Golgotha, in the Aramaic-Jewish language, means "place of the skull". Jesus was crucified at the place of the skull—the intellect was crossed out—that Christ, Truth, might become all in all.

In Matthew 27, Verse 34, *When the procession reached Golgotha, and before Jesus was put on the cross the Roman soldiers offered him wine mingled with myrrh.* It was customary to give those who were to be crucified a drink of wine medicated with a powerful narcotic to dull the terrible pain. *But He (Jesus) received it not.* (Mark 15:23) He chose to be in full control of all His faculties. On Friday morning at the "third hour."(nine o'clock) the crosses were raised. Jesus was in the middle, with a thief on each side.

The Roman soldiers had stripped Jesus of His garments and divided them. However, when they saw His coat, they agreed not to tear it but to cast lots for its possession. The coat, or seamless robe as it is generally called, was a beautiful and valuable garment, *Without seam, woven from the top throughout.* John 19:23

We are told in the Gospel Story (John 19:19) that Pilate placed a sign reading, "Jesus Nazarenus Rex Judaeorem" on Jesus' cross, and this is translated in the authorized version to mean, "Jesus of Nazareth, the King of the Jews."

The initials, INRI, placed upon the cross represent the names of the four elements in Hebrew: *Iam*, water; *Nour*, fire; *Rauch*, spirit or vital air; and *Iabeshah*, earth. Therefore, the four letters INRI, placed over the cross of Jesus the Christ, represent composite man. These are the four elements of our physical world of which our body is composed.

The metaphysical interpretation of the cross itself, not necessarily the Crucifixion cross, is that the vertical stroke represents the oneness of God, of the Godhead in general. It also symbolizes power descending upon mankind from above, or in the opposite direction, the yearning of mankind toward higher things. In the horizontal stroke, on the other hand, we see the earth in which life flows evenly and everything moves on the same plane.

In the sign of the cross, God and earth are combined

and are in harmony. From two simple lines a complete sign has been evolved. The cross is by far the earliest of all signs, and is found everywhere. The material of which the cross is formed is looked upon as being essential elements in its symbolism. A gold cross symbolizes illumination; a silver cross, purification, a cross of base metals, humiliation; and a cross of wood, aspiration.

The crucifixion symbolizes the crossing out of all that belongs to the mortal consciousness in order that the way be made for the coming forth of the Christ Self. The victory which we gain over the lower nature is something which must be achieved eventually by each one of us, a time when the lesser is sacrificed for the greater.

This is the real lesson of Good Friday; that the cross we take up in imitation of Jesus the Christ is the conquest of the lower nature. We should find our weak points and conquer them by knowing the Presence of God right where the undesirable traits seem to be. If we do this, we shall understand and enter into the glory of the Resurrection, and the freedom from slavery to our lower nature. It is not easy to "die" to the self—to our bad habits—to our own self-seeking. Each time we turn from a form of material sense, it is a kind of death, but the kind that precedes the resurrection.

This "dying" of the lower that the higher may be brought to birth is one of the deepest mysteries of the Cosmic Process.

Jesus said, Take up thy cross, and follow Me.
                                        Matthew 16:24

7

The Fourth Initiation . . . concluded
Seven Last Words . . . Seven Last Steps

Jesus's seven last words on the cross symbolize steps that must be taken in the final overcoming of the mortal mind. No one Gospel records all of the seven words. Each gives either one or three of them, and Bible scholars have arranged them in sequential order.

During the first three hours after Jesus was placed on the cross, He spoke three times. In these words He fulfilled His entire obligation to man; first, by forgiving His enemies; second, by promising mercy to the repentant sinner; and third, by discharging His responsibility to His mother.

The seven last words of Jesus are actually seven sayings. However, a word could describe each one.

The first word, and the first and most important step that we must take in the final overcoming is FORGIVENESS.

We read in Luke 23:33, 34:

And when they were come to the place which is called Calvary, there they crucified Him and the malefactors, one on the right hand and the other on the left, then said Jesus, "Father, forgive them for they know not what they do."

Jesus' first actual word in this, the final step of the Fourth Initiation, was "Father," a recognition of a higher power. Here again was the example. In the beginning of anything, we think on God. This recognition is basic and primary in any demonstration, in any advance. It must come first.

Father, forgive them for they know not what they do.

Jesus left us a perfect example of love and forgiveness. He forgave all who mistreated Him. His mastery in rising above the natural tendency to resent persecution came from the all-powerful Christ love that He expressed in His life.

Forgive us our debts, as we forgive our debtors.
Matthew 6:12

In these words, Jesus again expressed an infallible Law of Mind, the law that one idea must be dissolved before another can take its place. We may be wondering why we have failed to get spiritual illumination or find the consciousness of spiritual substance, or why love and companionship have not come to us. Perhaps the reason is here, a lack of room for the true thoughts because other thoughts fill our mind. We should search our mind carefully for unforgiving thoughts.

To hold in remembrance our own or another person's "sins" is to create an imperfect, distorted pattern from which we are fashioned.

Our forgiving everyone includes forgiving ourselves. We must forgive ourselves every "sin," every sense of separation from God. This is the major tragedy of human experience. It is, of course, rooted in ego. We try to live without God. We act as though we had a life of our own; as though we were separate from God and from other people. This feeling of separation, and the resulting feeling of guilt, causes us to be emotionally, mentally, and/or physically ill.

There is always something of a sense of loneliness that follows the doing of what we know to be wrong. We realize this especially when we have wronged one for whom we really care. Though our friend may not be aware of what we have done, we feel there is a barrier between our friend and some part of ourselves. We cannot respond to his friendship as we did before; we may even avoid him.

How much more, as we think of our relationship to God, does the sense of separation make itself felt. We are thrown back upon ourselves, living upon our own meager resources. We were never meant to face life alone.

The Bible abounds with passages about forgiveness and love. When the Scribes and Pharisees were condemning the fallen woman, Jesus said:

> *He that is without sin among you, let him cast the first stone,* John 8:7

The Prodigal Son was forgiven and the unforgiving brother was chided. Nowhere in the Bible can we find a petition for forgiveness that was not given.

Jesus admonished us to be loving when he said, *A new commandment I give you, that ye love one another; even as I have loved you.* (John 13:34) And in another passage, *To him who loves much, much is forgiven.* Luke 7:47

Most persons want to forgive and be forgiven, but too many are unwilling to take the first step. Why is it that we can find excuses for our anger against our neighbor, and yet we refuse to admit the same excuses when our neighbor is angry with us? We say that others would forgive us if they understood, and that the only reason they are angry with us is because "they do not understand." Why doesn't this work the

other way too? Can we not be as ignorant of their
motives as we say they are ignorant of ours?

*Jesus said, Judge not by appearances, but judge
righteous judgment.*   John 7:24

Can we look into their hearts? How little we know
of their motives, their background, their good faith,
the circumstances surrounding their actions.

In Matthew 6:14, 15, we read:

*For if ye forgive men their trespasses, your heav-
enly Father will also forgive you; but if ye forgive
not men their trespasses, neither will your Father
forgive your trespasses.*

The only way to experience forgiveness is to forgive
someone else. Through forgiveness of ourselves and
others, we cleanse our minds so that we are perfect
channels for the richness of God's love.

Jesus knew that unforgiveness is a destructive emotion based on a lack of understanding. Persons who are
unjust to us *"Know not what they do."*

The second word is "MERCY."

The two thieves who were crucified with Jesus represent the human belief in duality, good and evil—past

and future. "Jesus in the midst" represents the steady poise of the I AM. The past is full of regrets and accusations, and this thief says to Jesus, *Art not thou the Christ? Save Thyself and us.* Luke 23:39

The other thief reprimanded him, saying that they indeed were receiving their just desserts, but that Jesus was an innocent man, and turning to Jesus the repentant man said, *Remember me when Thou cometh into Thy Kingdom.* Luke 23:42

And Jesus said the second word:

Today shalt thou be with me in paradise.
Luke 23:43

So Jesus, with tender mercy, receives the penitent thief. This criminal, whose hand has been against every man's, in his last moments asked for consideration and was assured that he would be with Jesus. Whenever we turn to our Christ Self and ask for help, it is always freely given.

The second word shows us that we must have mercy, compassion, empathy. We must have the kind of love known as "agape." Agape is the love God has for us. God loves us, not because we are always lovable, but because we need love.

In Greek, the language in which the New Testament was written, there are three words for love, each with a different meaning: eros, philia, and agape. Eros means attraction to another person because of his/her attractiveness; the object of the love is the source of love.

Philia is an attraction to another person because of a mutual interest or concern. It arises between two people who like the same things, the same people.

Agape, unlike the other two kinds of love, does not depend upon the loveableness of the other person or upon shared interests. It arises out of a recognition of the need of the other person for love, for interest, and for fellowship; and it arises out of a recognition of our need to love. This is a love which expresses itself in action; we do something about it. It is not necessarily accompanied by emotion or sentiment.

To give the sharpest definition possible to agape, Jesus chose an example in which no elements of eros or philia are mixed. He said, *Love your enemies—do good to them that hate you.* (Luke 6:27) We still, with agape, would feed our enemies when they are hungry, help them out of a difficult situation, save their lives. We do not need to like a person or to be attacted to him, but we must have agape; we must wish him well.

In reply to Jesus' declaration, *Love thy neighbors as thyself*, a lawyer asked Him, *And who is my neighbor?* (Luke 10:27-36) Jesus gave the man an illustration that has become classic; the Parable of the Good Samaritan. The Samaritans and the Jews were hardly on speaking terms; but when the Samaritan, going down the road, saw a Jew lying injured at the hands of thieves, he took care of him. He responded to the need that came to his attention; he had compassion.

Day after day our paths cross those of people in need, with needs of various kinds. The lonely girl at the office needs companionship and a show of interest. A man at a party who feels shy and self-conscious needs to be drawn out. A fellow worker who feels insecure in his/her job needs to be encouraged and helped; the woman who recently moved in down the street has no friends and needs a visit. Our children, our husband or wife, our family, need our love when they seem to deserve it the least.

Pure agape love is giving with no expectation of return. If we do expect return, this is the wrong motive for helping others, and as Jesus said, *They have their reward.* When there is response from the other person, the chief joy should be that this grace has come to them, that the other person is better for their response. We must "love or perish." God has created us to love. To the extent we cut ourselves off from people, to the extent we do not love people, to that extent we are dead.

God has given His love fully to us, and no matter how many mistakes we have made, He says,

Today (now) thou shalt be with me in paradise.

The third word is "RESPONSIBILITY."

John 19:26-27:

When Jesus, therefore, saw His mother, and the disciple standing by, whom he loved, he saith unto His mother, "Woman, behold thy Son", then saith He to the disciple, "Son, behold thy mother".

Jesus addressed these words to Mary and the Disciple John, Love, who were standing near the cross. In this way, He fulfilled His responsibility to His mother. Tradition says that John cared for Mary for the remainder of her life. Jesus' action reminds us that it is our duty to provide for those who have a right to expect provision from us. Jesus taught right human relationships, that we should discharge our human responsibilities willingly and lovingly as a definite part of our spiritual unfoldment.

Responsibilities are important always; but most important when we are on the path. No one can ever be free from responsibilities until they are fulfilled. If our responsibilities sometimes seem too much, we should remember that Jesus said,

Come unto me, all ye that labour and are heavy burdened, and I will give thee rest, Matthew 11:28

We are told in the fifty-fifth Psalm to, *Cast thy burden upon the Lord.* Many passages in the Bible state that the battle is God's, not man's, and that man is to *Stand still and see the salvation of the Lord.* (Exodus 13:14) All that we need to do is to do that which is at hand, without undue expectation of reward and without fear, and leave the results to God.

Jesus fulfilled His responsibility to His mother through John, through Love. When we love, then our duties and responsibilities are lightened and are fulfilled. We have "cast our burdens on the Christ within."

Responsibility is often meant to denote duty, something imposed upon one from the outside. But responsibility, in its true sense, is an entirely voluntary act; it is our response to the needs, expressed or unexpressed, of another. To be responsible means to be able and ready to respond. The loving person responds. Our "response ability," our ability to respond, is from the center of our Being.

If we feel overly responsible for a person, we need to trust the God within him to care for him and guide him. This trusting is not a passive thing, but an active dynamic Faith that God is in charge. When it is time that our responsibilities should depart from us, we bless them and let them go, trusting the God within them to perfect right action.

It is the same with all human responsibility. We must turn them all over to Love. For whatever we love becomes a joy and not a burden. Let us give our responsibilities to love as we are told in the third word. In this way we are guided humanly to fulfill our responsibilities perfectly.

> *Come unto me all ye that are heavy-burdened, and*
> *I will give thee rest.* Matthew 11:28

Jesus was to be on the cross for three more hours, from noon until shortly after three in the afternoon. During these hours there was "darkness" over the whole land. Jesus was silent until just before three o'clock. At that time He uttered a cry of desolation and physical anguish.

Mark 15:34

> *And at the ninth hour, Jesus cried with a loud*
> *voice saying, "Eloi, Eloi, lama sabachthani?"*
> *Which is, being interpreted, "My God, My God,*
> *why has Thou forsaken Me?"*

So the fourth word could be "HUMAN HELPLESSNESS."

One of the features of the Fourth Initiation is that we are left completely alone. We feel cut off from all outside help, even from God. No one can become fully a saviour of men nor sympathize perfectly with all human suffering, unless he has faced and conquered pain

and fear and death unaided except by the aid he draws
from the God within. He must know the pangs of despair felt by the human soul when there is darkness on
every side.

My God, My God, why hast Thou forsaken Me? In
that uttermost loneliness, Jesus finds Himself. Losing
the God without, He finds the God within. For when
the darkness comes down, and nothing can be seen,
then arises the light of the Spirit in the human heart.
This lesson is that the true center of Divine Life lies
within and not without.

As the last loneliness descends on Jesus, He feels
Himself forsaken and alone, yet never is the Father
nearer to the Son than at the moment when the Soul
feels Himself forsaken. For as He touches the lowest
depth of sorrow, the hour of His triumph begins to
dawn. For now He learns that He must Himself
become the God to whom He cries, and by feeling the
last pang of separation, He finds the eternal unity.

There may be times when, in the face of overwhelm-
ing difficulty or apparently hopeless failure, we feel
that life has lost its meaning; and in the degree that we
have been trying to serve God faithfully, we are hope-
lessly at a loss, because it is God Himself that has
seemed to fail us. "Why," we say, "should this happen

to me? Does God really care?'' We feel absolutely helpless and forsaken.

At times like this, we are mercilessly prevented
from obtaining any outside help or relief whatsoever.
To human sense, all is lost: an ''incurable'' disease, an
''incurable'' financial problem, absolute rejection, or
some other seemingly desperate situation.

Crisis brings us face to face with our own inadequacy,
and our inadequacy, in turn, leads us to the inexhaust-
ible sufficiency of God. All great men and women have
known this: George Washington praying in the snow
at Valley Forge; Abraham Lincoln saying, ''When there
is no place else to go, we go to our knees.'' This is the
''power'' of human helplessness.

When achievement comes because of our helplessness linked to God's power, it has a rightness about it
that no amount of self-inspired striving can have. Fur-
thermore, when achievement comes in this way, it
does not bear in it the seeds of increasing egocentricity
that success sometimes brings. Because we know that
the ideas flow to us from God and not our little selves,
we can be objective about our good fortune or ability.

True creativity seems to come out of the pit of life
rather than the high places. Creativity is the ability to
put old material into new form. And it is only when
old molds and old ways of doing things are forcibly
broken up by need or suffering, compelling us to re-

group, to rethink, to begin again, that the creative process starts to flow.

When our periods of darkness and doubt come, when we feel that even God has forsaken us, we should remember that Jesus passed through a similar period. We should remember that it was momentary for Him and it will be for us, if we keep our mind "stayed on God." We may be inadequate, helpless, but God is very adequate!

The fifth word is "LONGING."

After this, Jesus, knowing that all things were now acomplished, that the scripture might be fulfilled, saith, "I thirst."   John 19:28

I thirst, the shortest of the seven words, symbolizes distress and an inner thirsting. In the Sermon on the Mount, Jesus said,

Blessed are they who do hunger and thirst after righteousness; for they shall be filled.
                                        Matthew 5:6

Righteousness means, in the Bible, not only right conduct, but right thinking, right use in every department of life. The Bible says if we *hunger and thirst after righteousness, we shall be filled*. And we are told in John 7:37, *If any man thirst, let him come unto me, and drink.*

Every now and then deep, unsatisfied longings well up within us. We may seem to have everything our heart can desire and ought to be perfectly satisfied. But still these vague dissatisfactions destroy our happiness. This is our "thirst after righteousness." Jesus said *Come unto me, and drink.* And in Revelation 7:16 we read, *They shall hunger no more, neither thirst no more.*

Our search for truth, for Spiritual illumination, must be an actual thirsting from the depth of our Being. When we truly thirst, this is all we think about; it is the only important thing in life, to have our thirst quenched. In a like manner, our soul is seeking the living waters of Truth with a deep longing, a thirst.

In John 4:14 we read:

But whosoever drinketh of the water that I shall give him shall never thirst; but the water that I shall give him shall be in him a well of water springing up into everlasting life.

This passage tells us that every longing of the human soul finds enduring satisfaction in the life-giving words of Jesus, representative of our own Christ Self. When we turn to the Center of our Being, we find a perpetual well of self-renewing inspiration. We never thirst again.

In the Gospel Story of the Crucifixion, apparently Jesus felt that the worst was over; and in the conviction that nothing could separate Him from His Father's love, He began to find rest and peace as death drew near.

By the cross stood a jar that contained a sour wine (vinegar) from which the Roman soldiers had drunk. When Jesus said, *I thirst* one of them took a sponge and, filling it with the liquid, raised it to Jesus' lips. Jesus accepted this simple act of mercy. Almost immediately He said, *It is finished.* John 19:30

When Jesus therefore had received the vinegar, He said, "It is finished."

This cry of Jesus is not just one of relief as if He were thankful that life's sorrowful journey was at an end. The Greek word "finished" means not simply "over and done with," but "brought to a complete fulfillment." It corresponds to a saying found in Jesus' remark, *I have finished the work which Thou gavest Me to do.* John 17:4

So the sixth word is "FULFILLMENT."

How strange this almost joyous word of fulfillment must have sounded to those who were standing by. Here was a young man who had not reached what we think of today as the "prime of life," coming, apparently, to an untimely end in the company of criminals, and yet, with His dying breath, declaring that He was content because He had fulfilled His life's destiny.

Jesus accepted all the responsibilities, perplexities, and anxieties that God's gift of freedom of choice carries with it. Like us, He had to make decisions in the face of changing conditions and opportunities.

The cry from the depths of His being in Gethsemane, *O, My Father, if it be possible, let this cup pass from me*, (Luke 22:42) tells us that, even as the crisis drew near, there was still a measure of uncertainty as to just how His Father's will for Him was to be realized.

As the years go by, and especially in these days of so much uncertainty, when it sometimes seems hardly worthwhile to make plans far ahead, do we not find ourselves asking what is the meaning of it all, and, in particular, what is the meaning of our own life?

We may have set our hearts on some limited achievement that seemed to lie within our own powers, yet because of a seeming failure, we now have a feeling of frustration, a sense of just being carried along against our own will, we know not where.

At times like this, it would be well to remember the old adage, "God has a plan for every man, and He has one for me!'' God has made us with a definite purpose in view. There can be no such thing as a misfit, or an unwanted or unneeded piece. It would not happen that God could create a Spiritual Entity such as we are, without having a special purpose in view, and this means that there is a special and particular place for each of us.

There is for each of us a perfect Self-Expression. There is a place which we can fill and no one else can fill, any more than they can fill the space we occupy physically; something that we can do, which no one else can do. This Perfect Idea is held in Divine Mind, awaiting our recognition.

Why are we here? To express God. ''God's will be done'' is the command we find running through all the scriptures.

Our perfect place is calling, and because we are really a spark of the Divine, we will never be content until we answer. Our heart's desire is the Voice of God.

St. Augustine wrote in the 5th Century, ''*For Thou hast formed us for Thyself, and our hearts are restless 'til they find repose in Thee.*''

This is the Call of God. And when God calls us to His Service, He pays all the expenses in whatever kind of coin—money, opportunity, introductions, knowledge, training, freedom, leisure, strength, and courage —all is furnished if we be about His business. In this way, we are brought to complete "fulfillment." Through the Truth, we are set free to manifest the man made in "His Image and likeness." Our freedom comes through fulfilling our destiny, bringing into manifestation the Divine Design of our life.

Jesus' suffering was now almost over. When we finally come to the place of knowing that every vestige of human effort is exhausted—that God is in control—our release is very near.

This release came to Jesus and it will come to us when the seventh or last word is spoken:

Father, into Thy hands I commend My Spirit, and having said thus, He gave up the ghost. Luke 22:46

The seventh word is "ACCEPTANCE."

Acceptance means a complete letting go and letting God. With this act of self-commitment, Jesus accepted the will of the Father.

There is a vast difference between acceptance and resignation. Acceptance is creative, positive. Resignation is sterile. Resignation is barren of faith in the love of God. It says, "Grievous circumstances have come to me. There is no escaping them. I am only one creature in a vast unknowable creation. I have no heart left even to rebel. So I'll just resign myself to what apparently is the will of God; I'll even try to make a virtue out of patient submission.'' So resignation lies down quietly in the dust of a universe from which God seems to have fled.

But acceptance says, ''I trust the good will, the love of God. I'll open my arms and my understanding to what He has allowed to come to me. Since I know that *All things work together for good, to those who love God* (Romans 8:28) I consent to this present situation with faith for what the future will bring.''

Acceptance leaves the door wide open to God's creative plan. This complete acceptance, this letting go and letting God, is the Law of Nonresistance. So long as we resist a situation, we will have it with us. If we run away from it, it will run after us! All of our problems are made of resistance. If we accepted everything which came our way, we would not suffer from pain.

The Doctrine of ''resist not evil'' is a great metaphysical secret. To the world, those who do not understand, it sounds like a milquetoast quality, the feeblest surrender to aggression. But in the light of the Jesus Christ revelation, it is seen to be superb, spiritual strategy. Antagonize any situation, and you give it power. Offer mental nonresistance, and it crumbles away in front of you. ''What we resist, persists.''

When Jesus spoke this last word, He *Gave up the ghost.* (John 19:30) At that moment, we read, *The veil of the temple was rent in two from the top to the bottom.*

At that moment the veil of sense consciousness was "rent" (torn) and Jesus came into consciousness of the body imperishable and eternal, the body temple "not made with hands, eternal in the heavens."

This rending of the veil is a complete letting go of all belief in the reality of material consciousness, and an awakening to the Light of Spirit. The final relinquishment of the soul to God is the final giving up of all human ambitions and aims. When this point is reached the soul enters into glory.

At the rending of the veil we read in Matthew 27:54, *An earthquake shook the earth and split the rocks,* and the Roman soldiers that were watching Jesus "feared greatly," and said, *Truly, this was the Son of God!*

Here then are the seven last words of Jesus and the seven last steps that we must take in our final overcoming. Jesus said, *I am the Way, the Truth and the Life, follow thou me!*

8

The Universal Law of Sacrifice

The Letting Go . . . *Release*

The Sabbath began at sunset on Friday and the Jews wanted the bodies of the three men taken down from the crosses before that time. To make sure that Jesus was dead, one of the Roman soldiers drove a spear into His side.

Joseph of Arimathea, a prominent Jew, a member of the Sanhedrin, and secretly a follower of Jesus, asked Pilate for Jesus' body for burial. The request was granted, and with the help of Nicodemus, Joseph wrapped the body in linen and laid it in a new tomb in his garden. A huge stone was then rolled to the entrance of the tomb. By the time the men had completed their ministration it was sunset and the Sabbath had begun.

Soon afterwards, the Chief Priest and Pharisees went to Pilate, saying, *Sir, we remember what that deceiver said, while he was yet alive, "After three days, I will rise again."* Matthew 27:62

Command therefore that the sepulchre be made sure until the third day, lest his disciples come by night, and steal Him away, and say unto the people, "He is risen from the dead," so the last error shall be worse than the first.

Pilate said unto them, "Ye have a watch; go your way, make it as sure as ye can."

So they went, and made the sepulchre sure, sealing the stone, and setting the watch.

The Story of Jesus continues after the Crucifixion with an incident hinted at, but not specifically mentioned in the Gospels. In the words of the Nicene Creed, *He then descended into hell.*

This immediate descent into hell, or limbo, might have several meanings. One meaning could be that no region of the universe He is to help would remain untrodden by Him, or to show that there are none too outcast to be reached by His all-embracing love.

In an individual sense, it could stand for a final liberation from the dark places in ourselves by bringing the light of full Christ Consciousness to bear on the unconscious mind. The presence of the Christ Light within is a liberating force.

The Crucifixion of Jesus became the foundation of the Christian doctrine of salvation by the blood of

Jesus. Christians generally believe that Jesus gave His blood on the cross as sacrifice for the sins of every person, and that when one accepts Him as the Saviour one is saved by His Blood. The Jews believed that sin was cleansed through sacrifice, that the blood of the slain animal on the altar cleansed man of sin.

The blood must not be eaten—it was given to God, for whom the altar stood. The Jewish people identified life with blood. Loss of blood meant death to them, so the blood became sacred. The blood belonged to God.

In order to show the parallel in the life of Christ to the Hebrew idea of blood sacrifice, Paul preached to the Jews that Jesus was the great once-and-for-all blood sacrifice and that no other blood sacrifice would ever be necessary.

We can understand this doctrine as applied to the Christ when we see it as a special manifestation of the Universal Law of Sacrifice. A reflection below of the pattern above, showing us, in a concrete human life what sacrifice means.

All the great religions of the world have said that the universe began by an act of sacrifice, and have incorporated the idea of sacrifice into their most solemn rites.

The Law of Sacrifice might perhaps more truly be called the Law of Manifestation or the Law of Love and of Life as symbolized by the Cross. This sacrifice is the secret of evolution. Through the perpetual sacrifice of

104 / Metanoia—A Transformational Journey

the One, all lives exist. This life is One, but it embodies itself in many forms. The Law of Growth of Life is that we increase by pouring forth and not by drawing from without; by giving, not by taking. Sacrifice, then in this primary meaning, is a thing of joy.

But the word *sacrifice* has come to be associated with suffering. The explanation is seen when we turn from the manifesting life to the forms in which it is embodied, and look at the question of sacrifice from the world of form.

While the life of Life is in giving, the life of form is in taking. The Law of Growth of form, the body for instance, is to take and assimilate that which the universe supplies. As the consciousness identifies itself with the form, regarding the form as itself, sacrifice takes on a painful aspect. To give, to surrender, to lose what has been acquired, is felt to threaten the form; therefore, the Law of Sacrifice becomes a law of pain, instead of a law of joy.

In order for us to take advantage of the atonement Jesus made for us, it is imperative that we follow Him. *Keep My Word*, He said. This means that we are to take on His ideas, speak His words, and do the things that He did. He set an example and He showed that whatever He urged others to do, He could and did do.

He taught love by showing love. He taught forgiveness by forgiving those who despitefully used Him.

His is the greatest service ever rendered to humanity for, through His "sacrifice," His "giving up" and "overcoming," He released the Christ Consciousness into the world.

We all recognize the advantage of group thought. It is much easier to hold ourselves in the true consciousness when we are with others who think as we do. It was the work of Jesus to establish in our race consciousness a spiritual center with which we all might become associated mentally.

There is a way by which the shadow of the Christ Life may fall on us all, and that is by doing every act as an act of sacrifice to God. When we perform every act not for our glory, but for the glory of God, when we surrender each day into God's keeping, we begin to live under the Law of Grace, the Law of Love, and are no longer subject to the Law of Cause and Effect.

By releasing each passing moment and each action to God, we let go of the past. We do not build up any sorrow nor do we build guilt, for God has purified that which is past. In order not to carry a burden from one day to the next, each night before going to sleep, release the day to God. Review the day in the presence of God, *For God requireth that which is past.*

In Ecclesiastes 3:15 we read, That which hath been is now, and that which is to be hath already been: and God requireth that which is past.

In this way we live fully and completely in the NOW and our response is a Spiritual response from the center of our being, not a subconscious reaction colored by our past.

Only one condition is needed in order that the Christ within may share His strength with us and that is our willingness to receive. There must be an opening from below as well as an outpouring from above. In this way we grow into the life of "the Beloved Son, and have the Glory of the Christ."

Each of us may work in this direction by making every act an act of sacrifice. By releasing each passing moment and each action to God, we no longer sow the seeds of cause that would create undesirable effects.

So the "blood atonement" is used to express a Spiritual Principle that has been introduced into the race mind through the purified Jesus. It is a Spiritual Principle, yet it manifests in mind and body in concrete form. Jesus became the way by which all who accept Him may "pass over" to the new consciousness—the Christ Consciousness. By His example, He opened a way which all who desire may demonstrate easily and quickly.

This Christ principle does not offer a partial salvation. We are told in Matthew 5:48, *Be ye therefore perfect, even as your Father in heaven is perfect.* This can mean nothing less than complete atonement, complete at-one-ment!

9

The Fifth Initiation

The Resurrection . . . *The Demonstration!*

The five initiations of the Master Jesus during His life in Palestine are known as the Birth, the Baptism, the Transfiguration, the Crucifixion, the Resurrection, and the Ascension. The Fifth Initiation is divided into two halves; the Resurrection and the Ascension. These five initiations set guideposts along the way of the Disciple. They exemplify the experience of the human soul through the five stages of its Spiritual journey from sense to soul to Spirit.

The story of the Resurrection is told in Luke 24:1–12:

Now upon the first day of the week, very early in the morning, they came unto the sepulchre, bringing the spices which they had prepared, and certain others with them.

And they found the stone rolled away from the sepulchre. And they entered in, and found not the body of the Lord Jesus.

And it came to pass, as they were much perplexed thereabout, behold, two men stood by them in shining garments: and they were afraid, they bowed down their faces to the earth.

They said to them, "Why seek ye the living among the dead?"

"He is not here, but is risen: remember how He spake unto you when He was yet in Galilee, saying, the Son of man must be delivered into the hands of sinful men, and be crucified, and the third day rise again."

And they remembered His words, and returned from the sepulchre, and told all these things unto the eleven, and to all the rest.

And their words seemed to them as idle tales, and they believed them not.

Then arose Peter, and ran unto the sepulchre: and stooping down, he beheld the linen clothes laid by themselves, and departed, wondering in himself at that which was come to pass.

Plato's doctrine was that the outward body and the material nature are the graves of the Divine Principle. Each person ascends to the Light when the "stone is rolled away." And what is the stone but materiality? It is essential in our preparation for the risen Christ to roll away the many stones in our lives, stones that entomb us, such as hatred, envy, dissension, impatience, unforgiveness, and materiality. It is the task of each one of us to remove any stone that is preventing the Christ within from coming forth into our life.

The Resurrection takes place in each of us every time we rise to the realization of the indwelling Christ. The graveclothes of mortal sense, which are thoughts of limitation, are then left in the tomb of matter. The Resurrection of Jesus the Christ is the symbol of the Resurrection of Truth in everything that lives. It is the Resurrection of reality from illusion, of life from death, of love from hate. It is the second coming—the coming of Truth in our own hearts.

Believe in the Resurrection? Who can doubt it? Who has not experienced something of the glory of it as they were lifted out of discouragement through faith, or regained health after sickness?

Ernest Holms writes in WORDS THAT HEAL TODAY, "We shall miss the most significant part of Jesus' teaching unless we believe in His resurrection, and through this revelation, in the resurrection of all."

Paul in the 15th Chapter of I Corinthians makes it clear that the Christian teaching would be "in vain" were it not for the resurrection from the dead. *If Christ has not been raised*, he says, *your faith is futile*.

The Resurrection Body is not a body which is "made with hands." It is not formed by experience. It is a body which belongs to the Christ Life; it is built of God, it is the "only begotten" of God.

> For we know that if our earthly house of this tabernacle were dissolved, we have a building of God, a house not made with hands, eternal in the heavens.   II Corinthians 5:1.

The Christian religion has been based on a belief in immortality as an individual. Jesus rose from the dead and passed from this plane to the next, retaining and carrying with Him those qualities and attributes which make up that personal screen of consciousness known as an individual.

Jesus recognized His identity in God as the Christ, the Son of God. We shall come into conscious recognition of the Christ Mind just as soon as we let go of the limitations of human sense.

Thinking on the Christ Story, two points stand out clearly. One is that the new life which the Risen Christ brings to men is not just ordinary, biological life alone. The second point is that the bestowal of this gift is the fruit of death. Die and come to life. This is the essence of the Story. It is like learning to float on the water. So long as we tense our muscles and try to hold our body upon the surface, we sink. But as soon as we surrender ourselves to the buoyancy (the invisible power) of the water, we relax and float.

In the familiar language of the Gospel:

Whosoever would save his soul shall lose it. But he that loses his soul shall find it. Matthew 10:39

Die and come to Life. Romans 11:15

Except a grain of corn fall into the ground and die. It remains alone, but if it dies, it brings forth much fruit. John 12:24

This is what the Resurrection is saying: the source of life, not ordinary life alone, but eternal life, is death itself; death to the self. The source of supreme joy is something which, at first sight, seems to be utter despair.

Only poetry and symbols can even attempt to describe the transformation that happens when we know that we can do nothing but let go and let God. To try to describe or imagine it is unnecessary. It is simply there, already given by the Grace of God!

Jesus said, I am the Resurrection and the Life: and he that believeth on Me, though he die, yet shall he live. John 11:25

We can use the power of the Resurrection on every appearance of imperfection, resurrecting the life essence within to its perfect estate. Call for the Resurrection and the Life of all dormant talents, gifts, and powers.

Call for the Resurrection and the Life of Perfection with these affirmations.

"I AM" THE RESURRECTION AND THE LIFE OF PERFECTION of every cell and atom of my body now made manifest!

"I AM" THE RESURRECTION AND THE LIFE OF PERFECTION of my finances now made manifest in my hands and use today!

"I AM" THE RESURRECTION AND THE LIFE OF PERFECTION of home . . . Relationships . . . Communication . . . Divine Order . . . (name what you wish to have resurrected) *now made Manifest!*

"I AM" the fullness of God's plan fulfilled right now and forever!

"I AM" is the word that heals!

Christ in us is the Resurrection and the Life. Whenever we have faith in ultimate good, we are proving the resurrecting power of Christ within us. Everytime we replace an angry, unkind impulse with a generous, uplifting thought or act, we are resurrected. Every comeback, every overcoming, every healing, every increase of Spiritual substance is a Resurrection.

We are told that if we follow in His footsteps, we will find the same place in the Father that He found.

If a man love Me, he will keep My Word: and My Father will love him, and We will come unto him and make Our abode with him.   John 14:23

If thou wouldst be perfect, follow thou Me.
                                        Matthew 19:21

10

The Victory Over Death
The Appearances of Jesus

During the forty days following His Resurrection, Jesus appeared to His followers on ten occasions. His Resurrection was not complete until His followers were convinced of the Resurrection. The Disciples were to continue the Christ ministry, and they had to be convinced that He still lived.

The appearances of Jesus are as much a part of Jesus' teaching as the three years of His ministry. These appearances verify the fact that we do "maintain a continuous stream of consciousness." As a result of His appearances after the Resurrection, the loyalty and faith of the Disciples were renewed and they became the leaders of a faithful and united group.

The Gospels give short accounts of Jesus' appearances and present facts that are vital to our spiritual unfoldment, for these appearances lead to the Ascension. Five of Jesus' appearances were on the day of the

Resurrection, and the first of them was to Mary Magdalene.

Mary Magdalene, out of whom Jesus cast seven demons, became one of His most devoted followers. The demons were said to be avarice, envy, sloth, anger, deceit, Spiritual pride, and blasphemy (denying God). This means that the Christ in us releases our soul from our mistaken ways of feeling and thinking. As the soul (Mary) is purified and lifted out of the bondage of the mistakes (demons), it (the soul) pours more and more devotion and service to the Christ in us, represented by Jesus.

In Luke 8:1–3, John 19:25, and John 20:11–18, we find Mary Magdalene among those following Jesus from place to place, ministering to Him. We see her by the cross and standing at the tomb weeping. Then the angels appear to her; next the risen Jesus reveals Himself to her, and she goes to tell the Disciples the glad news.

In John 20:11–13 we read:

But Mary stood without at the sepulchre weeping: and as she wept, she stooped down, and looked into the sepulchre. And seeth two angels in white sitting, the one at the head, and the other at the feet, where the body of Jesus had lain. And they said unto her, "Woman, why weepest thou?" She saith unto them, "Because they have taken away my Lord, and I know not where they have laid Him."

How often do we feel that *They have taken away my Lord, and I know not where they have laid Him*? When we are making a transition from one stage of development to another, we often feel this sense of loss at leaving the familiar belief, or form.

Mary's weeping was the human reaction of grief over the death of a loved one, and added to her grief was the fear that someone had stolen Jesus' body. Jesus was standing nearby, but Mary's eyes were filled with tears and at first she did not recognize Him. When He asked why she wept, she thought He was the gardener.

Then Jesus saith unto her, "Mary"; she turned herself (she looked to the Divine) *and saith unto Him, "Rabboni"' which is to say "Master."*

Jesus saith unto her, "Touch me not; for I am not yet ascended unto the Father; but go unto my brethren, and say unto them, 'I ascend unto my Father and your Father, and my God and your God.'"   John 20:17

The thoughts of sorrow are dissipated by a denial of their reality of power to affect the mind of the Son of God. *"Touch Me not!"*

The second appearance of Jesus was to the other women who had come with Mary Magdalene to anoint His body.

And behold, Jesus met them saying, "All hail,"
and they came and took hold of his feet, and wor-
shipped Him. Then saith Jesus unto them, "Fear
not: Go tell My brethren that they depart into Ga-
lilee, and there shall they see Me."

Matthew 28:9, 10

Another appearance of Jesus was to Peter (Faith), Luke 24:34, *The Lord is risen indeed, and hath ap-*
peared to Simon (Peter). On the same day toward evening, Jesus appeared to two Disciples on the road to Emmaus. The two Disciples with sad and anxious hearts were discussing the incidents of the past two days, when a stranger joined them and asked about their distress. They were surprised that anyone who lived in Jerusalem had not heard of the Crucifixion of Jesus of Nazareth. Luke 24:19–26

Art thou a stranger in Jerusalem, and hast not
known the things which are come to pass there in
these days?

And He said unto them, "What things?"

And they said unto Him, "concerning Jesus of Nazareth, which was a prophet mighty in deed and word before God and all people and how the Chief Priests and our rulers delivered Him to be condemned to death, and crucified Him."

But we trusted that it had been He which should have redeemed Israel: and beside all this, today is the third day since these things were done.

Then he said unto them, "O fools, and slow of heart to believe all that the prophets have spoken: Ought not Christ to have suffered these things, and to enter into His glory?"

When they sat down together to eat, *Jesus took bread, and blessed it, and brake it, and gave to them.*

And then we read, *Their eyes were opened and they knew Him; and He vanished out of their sight.*
                                                    Matthew 24:30, 31

The two Disciples hurried to Jerusalem to tell the good news to the other Disciples. But before they could tell their news, they were greeted with the glad tidings, *"The Lord has risen indeed."* Then they told of their experience with the risen Saviour.

Jesus' fifth appearance was in the evening, and ten of the Apostles (Thomas was not there) were together in a room in Jerusalem. The door was closed.

Suddenly, Jesus came and stood in the midst, and saith unto them, "Peace be unto you." And when he had said this, he showed unto them his hands and his side. The disciples therefore were glad when they saw the Lord.

Jesus said to them again, "Peace be unto you: As the Father hath sent Me, even so send I you,"

John 20:19–21.

The ten Disciples went quickly to tell Thomas of Jesus' appearance. To him the news seemed too good to be true, and he said,

Except I shall see in his hands the print of the nails, and put my hand into his side, I will not believe.   John 20:25.

Thomas (Understanding) was the doubting one. He had to have proof. A week after the Resurrection, Thomas was given the proof he required, for the eleven Disciples were together on Sunday evening when Jesus appeared. He invited Thomas to see His hands, feel His side, *"And be not faithless, but believing."* John 20:22

Then Thomas exclaimed, "My Lord and my God!"

And Jesus said, "Because thou hast seen me, thou hast believed; blessed are they that have not seen, and yet have believed."   John 20:28, 29

Thomas represents the understanding that, in the natural man, is dubious until it is convinced by proof. Jesus respected the demand of Thomas for physical evidence and gave it to him. Nevertheless, He commended those who believe even before they see the proof. When understanding becomes Spiritually quickened, it becomes intuition, quick, instinctive knowing with no need for proof.

The day of the seventh appearance of Jesus is not known. It took place early one morning at the Sea of Galilee, where seven of the disciples had been fishing all night. Just as day was breaking, Jesus appeared on the shore. From a distance, those in the boat did not know that it was He. Calling to them, Jesus asked if they had caught any fish, and when they replied in the negative, He said:

"Cast thy net on the right side of the boat, and ye shall find". They cast therefore, and now they were not able to draw it for the multitude of fishes
                                                        John 21:6

Again, Jesus is saying that we must have a complete change of mind. We work long and hard in the darkness (night) of human understanding and gain very little but once the Christ Mind is perceived and obeyed, the net is cast on the "right side" and success immediately follows.

John (Love) was the first to recognize Jesus. "It is the Lord," he said, and then the impetuous Peter (Faith) jumped into the sea and swam to shore. There they found prepared a meal of fish and bread, which Jesus invited them to eat. The bread and fish that Jesus provided on the shore represent the supply of Spirit for the needs of the body. Not only does the Father provide for us in the invisible world, but in the visible world too. He provides the "loaves and fishes" needed by us in our everyday living.

In John 21:15–21 we read:

So when they had dined, Jesus saith to Simon Peter, "Lovest thou Me more than these?" He (Peter) saith unto Him, "Yea, Lord; thou knowest that I love thee."

Jesus saith unto him, "Feed My sheep." He saith unto him again the second time, "Simon, Son of Jonas, lovest thou Me?" He saith unto him, "Yea, Lord; thou knowest that I love Thee." He said unto Him "Feed my sheep."

He saith unto him the third time, "Simon, Son of Jonas, lovest thou me?" Peter was grieved because he said unto Him the third time, "Lovest thou me?" And he said unto him, "Lord, Thou knowest all things: Thou knowest that I love Thee." Jesus saith unto him, "Feed my sheep."

Jesus is saying to Peter that true faith must be rooted in a love for the Christ and a willingness to serve Him by serving others. We demonstrate our faith by serving others and therefore serving the Christ. "Words without works are dead!" Jesus said, *Feed My sheep!*

In the scriptures we read, *"If you have done it unto the least of these, you have done it unto me."* Jesus said three times, *Feed My sheep!*

After his protestations of love to Jesus, Peter turned and saw John who was following them. Peter said, *Lord, and what shall this man do?* Peter had his instructions and he wanted to be sure that John received his orders too.

Jesus' reply was a rebuke. *If I will that he tarry till I come, what is that to thee? Follow thou Me.* John 21:22 The highest duty of each of us is to follow the Christ. We should do our appointed work and not concern ourselves with what another does or fails to do. Our faith faculty (Peter) is dictatorial at times. We should put it under the dominion of the Christ, who alone knows how each faculty should function.

Jesus came to them and spake unto them, saying, "All authority hath been given unto me in heaven and on earth. Go ye therefore and make disciples of the nations, baptizing them in the name of the Father and of the Son and of the Holy Spirit: Teaching them to observe all things whatsoever I commanded you: Lo, I am with you always, even unto the end of the world." Matthew 28:18–20

In our Spiritual nature, we do have authority over all things (heaven and earth). In the consciousness of our Christ Self, we are to teach His Word. The only way we can do this is to be continually aware that we labor in HIS name (nature) and that He is always with us.

Jesus instructed His Disciples to:

Go ye into all the world and preach the Gospel to the whole creation. He that believeth and is baptized shall be saved; but he that disbelieveth shall be condemned, and these signs shall accompany them that believe:

In My name shall they cast out demons; they shall speak with new tongues: They shall take up serpents, and if they drink any deadly thing, it shall no wise hurt them: They shall lay hands on the sick, and they shall recover. Mark 16:15–18

Since this is the story of our own unfoldment, we are to preach the Gospel to every part of us (the whole creation) and believe and be baptized by using cleansing denials (water) and words of affirmative power (fire). Then we are told that we shall cast out devils (our flesh habits, conditioned reflexes, compulsion, etc.), speak with new tongues (our words will truly have power), pick up serpents (lift up our sense consciousness); deadly things will not harm us, and we shall heal the sick.

All this is promised to all who BELIEVETH AND ARE BAPTIZED.

The eighth and ninth appearances of Jesus are not recorded in the Gospels but are mentioned in Paul's Epistle to the Corinthians, *Then he appeared to James; then to all the Apostles,* I Corinthians 15:7

The last and tenth appearance was to the Eleven just before the Ascension.

And being assembled together with them, he charged them not to depart from Jerusalem, but to wait for the promise of the Father which, said he, "Ye heard from Me: For John indeed baptized with water; but ye shall be baptized in the Holy Spirit not many days hence." They therefore, when they

*were come together asked him saying, "Lord, dost
Thou at this time restore the Kingdom to Israel?"*

*And he said unto them, "It is not for you to know
times or seasons which the Father hath set within
His own authority. But ye shall receive power,
when the Holy Spirit is come upon you: and ye
shall be My witnesses both in Jerusalem, and in all
Judea and Samaria, and unto the uttermost part of
the earth."*   Acts 1:4–8

Here is Jesus' promise of the descent of power from on
high to those who are faithful to Him. Only then can
we fulfill the provisions of what is sometimes called
the Great Commission, namely, to be HIS witnesses
to ourselves, to everyone, everywhere.

Jesus commanded the Disciples that they should not
depart from Jerusalem, but should "wait." There are
times when the hardest thing in the world is to do
nothing, yet there are times when that is the only
thing to do. There are some things we can work for;
there are other things we can only wait for. For instance, we can work for a living; we can only wait for
the spring. Life is a composition of activity and
passivity. We have become experts in activity and are
only novices in passivity.

Yet in religion there is a primary place for passivity;

it is the mood in which the soul is receptive to promptings from above. A person who waits upon God is like a man waiting for the sun, expectant, sure, ready to begin his day.

Lord wilt Thou at this time restore again the Kingdom of Israel?

It is interesting to note that Jesus did not answer this question; He corrected it. He said, *It is not for you to know the times or the season, which the Father hath put in his own power. But ye receive power . . . and be witnesses unto me.* He shifted the emphasis from speculation about the future to demonstration in the present.

When times are hard, it is always a temptation to some people to dream about the future, and to project into the future all the things they long for, yet lack in the present. Jesus was of a different mind. *Be witnesses unto Me*, He said. In other words, begin now! Let the world see a demonstration of what the power of God can do when it works through those who trust in God!

He would say the same to us. Stop speculating about the future and begin to live in the NOW. Now God (our Good) is with us, as us, not sometime in the future when we have a new car, a new home, a better job, and so forth. God is, our good is, NOW! Our task, according to Jesus, is to transform the present by witnessing to the Christ, by living up to the highest in us, and glorifying our good.

Jesus purposely kept His body on the physical plane for forty days in order to be with His Disciples and to complete His instructions to them. Forty, in the minds of the ancient Hebrew writers, was a four-square number suggesting the idea of a foundation for something that was to follow.

At the end of the forty days' time, Jesus made His final demonstration in His Atonement (at-one-ment) with the Father, and the Ascension took place.

11

The Fifth Initiation . . . concluded

The Ascension . . .
The Spiritualization of the Bodies

On Thursday of the sixth week after Easter (forty days after the Resurrection) many churches celebrate the Feast of the Ascension. According to the scriptures, on that day, Jesus commissioned His Apostles to preach the Gospel to all nations; then, having blessed them, He was lifted up before their eyes, *"And a cloud received Him out of their sight".* Acts 1:9.

And when he had said these things, as they were looking, He was taken up, and a cloud received Him out of their sight.

And while they were looking steadfastly into heaven, as He went, behold two men stood by them in white apparel: who also said

"Ye men of Galilee, why stand ye looking into heaven? This Jesus, who was received up from you

129

*into heaven, shall so come in like manner as ye
beheld Him going into heaven.''*

Then they returned unto Jerusalem.   Acts 1:9–12

They looked steadfastly toward heaaven. This is symbolic of us when we keep our mind stayed on God, on
Good. People instinctively look up when they are ex-
pecting good. There is something wonderful always
about looking up, keeping a high watch. We, like the
Disciples, are not yet able to abide with the Christ. Yet
even before we make the final attainment, we may
walk in the footsteps of Jesus the Christ. Each day
presents a chance for us to go a little farther along the
way that leads to eternal life. In order to complete the
outline necessary for the understanding of the Resurrection and the Ascension, we must see what we can
do to hasten our higher evolution.

The Essenes believed that the immortal part of man
is held within the body as though imprisoned.
Through disciplining the flesh, releasing the mind and
heart from all worldliness, and dedicating the life to
good works, the soul could be liberated and could
finally ascend.

Our physical body is in a constant state of flux. Its
minute particles are being continually renewed. We
are composed of the food we eat, the liquids we drink,
the air we breathe, and the particles drawn from our
physical surroundings. We can purify our body by

choosing its materials well, making it a purer vehicle through which to express. For this reason, part of the ancient religious disciplines had to do with diet and rules of cleanliness, such as taught by the Essenes.

We are told in Job 19:26, *Yet in my flesh shall I see God*. Do we see Him there? We could. The flesh can become the instrument which God meant it to be.

For too long we have been taught that the body is a miserable thing which we have to carry around with us, rather than the Temple of the Living God, the instrument through which God speaks and expresses.

Truly, as the Psalmist sang, *We are fearfully and wonderfully made!* Psalms 138:14

Every tiny cell in our body is an individual unit, living an individual life.

We could describe what goes on in the body by making a picture of a submarine. Let us think of our cells as the men in the submarine. The captain of the submarine is the only one who can look through the periscope and see the outside world. They must act upon what he, the captain, tells them.

You, the reasoning you, are the captain of your body. The men in the submarine are your cells. They cannot see outside. They must accept your word implicitly. You are the only one who can look through the periscope. The cells can be fed a diet of frustration, of fear, of discouragement. We can blame them for not being efficient, or we can praise them and glorify them so they sing with joy.

Talk to your cells. Praise your cells. Tell your cells that you believe in them and have confidence in them and in their ability to do their work." Say to your cells, "I have faith in you. I believe that God gave you the power to do your work." The body is sensitive; it registers every thought and feeling. Watch how many times we say something derogatory about some part of it. You may be giving it constant negative suggestions. It will follow them as faithfully as it will follow affirmative ones.

Bless your body always. Speak no word of condemnation about it. Praise and bless every cell, calling upon each cell for its perfect response. In talking to your cells, remember they have no reasoning intelligence. They do not talk back to you except in the way of discomfort when they are too discouraged to do their work.

They do not say to you, "It isn't so." They have instinctive intelligence, but not reasoning intelligence. They take your word and you speak the word.

Jesus proclaimed, I am the Light of the world.
                                            John 8:12

He was speaking of the inner light which gives life and intelligence to all creation. When we affirm "I

AM'' with our thought centered upon Spirit, we quicken the life flow in the body and awaken the sleepy cells. Such affirmations clear up congested areas of the organism and restore the circulation to its normal state—health.

When we turn our attention within and give ourselves up wholly to Spirit, we are quickened with a life and intelligence of superexcellence.

Every good gift and every perfect gift is from above, and cometh down from the Father of Lights. James 1:17

That was the true light, which lighteth every man that cometh into the world. John 1:19

The body of our desires (emotions) also changes. Materials for the emotional body are expelled and drawn in by the play of the desires, arising from the feelings, passions and emotions. If these are coarse, the materials built into the desire body are also coarse. In proportion as we become unselfish in our wishes, feelings and emotions, as we make our love for those around us less selfish and grasping, we are purifying the body or our emotions.

Charis love is the great purifier. It is the Christ love, the love that releases, and not the love that possesses; the love that bestows, and not the love that receives. Charis love is unconditional love.

Try charis love in some very simple way. Write that letter to the person to whom you have never wanted to speak again. Meet someone halfway for whom you have long held a grudge. Look over your opinions, what you are for, and what you are against. Can you say that your attitude toward the people around you is the attitude of a truly enlightened, patient person? Are you demanding too much from those who cannot give? Do you irritate too easily? Do you sadden too quickly? Are you too easily hurt? Do you have self-pity? Are you driven by too great an ambition?

Take one simple problem and go to work on it with charis love. Then watch what happens. You will find that this simple decision begins the gradual transmutation of your total life. One small change for the better, and all of you will be better. Whenever we cling to the Divine Law of Love, there is light; and where there is light, there is peace and healing.

The Christ within is always declaring, I am the light of the world: he that followeth Me shall not walk in the darkness, but shall have the Light of Life! John 8:12

The body of our intellect is also being built and rebuilt by our thoughts and words, by imagination, reason, judgment, by the use of all mental powers. There should be a constant activity of Truth going on all the time. We could train ourselves to have some area of consciousness active in Truth. In this way we "abide" in the Presence.

Many mystics have made a prayer, a mantra, an affirmation, a Bible quotation, the center of their life. The affirmation continues in the mind even when conversing with others or attending to the business of living. This is not "vain repetition," but is a way of stilling the mind and keeping the mind "stayed on God." It is a way of taking the energy and attention off the incessant "rooftop chatter" of the mind.

Almost everyone, to some degree or another, is afflicted with this mad carnival of mind chatter, this robber of peace and contentment. This repetitous mind chatter manifests as patterns of fear and anxiety. Instead of being open to the beauty of existence here and now, we are too often obsessed about the mistake we made yesterday, what will happen tomorrow, and on and on.

As we focus our attention on words of Truth, on a mantra, on a prayer, on whatever is right and natural for us, the racket of our mind slowly unwinds and begins to settle. In this concentration, there is the cultivation of a center of quiet.

Almost every religion and Spiritual path reflects the idea of repetition as a basis for its practice. What one considers to be monotonous soon becomes uplifting. Conscious repetition brings us to a state of presentness which enriches our relationship to the world and encourages spontaneity.

The ideal for our three body vehicles is that they act as a unit. The three must be one, coordinated and aligned, so that they become a perfect instrument for the expressing of the Christ Life. We become conscious of the higher vibrations as we purify our earthly vehicles—the physical body, the emotional body, and the mental body.

We are living in an ocean of Light, of Love, that surrounds us at all times. As the sun floods the earth with its radiance, so does the God Life enlighten us all. We shut this light out of our consciousness by our selfishness, our heartlessness, our impurity, our intolerance; but it shines on us nonetheless, pressing against our self-built walls with gentle, strong persistence.

Only when we consent will God take over, though He be "everywhere present." God respects our individuality, and will not enter our consciousness until we give welcome.

Behold, I stand at the door and knock (Revelations 3:20) is the attitude of Spiritual Intelligence towards the evolving human soul—not in lack of sympathy, but in deepest wisdom. We are not to be compelled; we are free. We are not a slave, but a God in the unfolding, and the growth cannot be forced, but must be willed from within.

Draw nigh to God, and He will draw nigh to you.
James 5:8

It is a comfort to know that we do not have to make the entire journey alone back to the Father. We read that when the Prodigal Son was coming back to his Father, *While he was yet afar off, his father saw him, and was moved with compassion. He ran and fell on his neck and kissed him.* Luke 15:20

The Superconscious Mind, the Christ, lifts up, regenerates both the subconscious and conscious minds, transforming them into the true image and likeness of God. We must lay aside forever the idea of serving two masters and look to the one Master, the Christ, the Spiritual Consciousness within. Jesus said that He came not to destroy the law, but that the law might be fulfilled through Him. It is the mission of every person born into the world to fulfill the Law of Being. The Christ within is always declaring:

I am the Light of the world. He that followeth Me shall not walk in darkness, but shall have the Light of Life. John 8:12

The mystic understands the Ascension not only as an historical event, but also as the unfolding of evolutionary processes on the plane of consciousness. Materially we grow in darkness toward the light;

Spiritually we grow in light toward the source of universal light, as symbolized by the Ascension.

> *Jesus said, Go to My brethren, and say unto them, "I ascend unto My Father, and your Father: and to My God, and your God"*   John 20:17

Jesus, our great teacher and wayshower, is saying to us, "What I can do you can do, you are as Divine as I am, we have the same Father God...follow me!"

An ascension is accomplished in the moment we hold in thought an experience, a feeling or a memory that raises the vibrations and makes us feel good about ourselves. Any time we allow ourselves to feel good about ourselves, we expand within our auric structure and we are lifted right up and out of ourselves. We ascend!

12

The Baptism of the Holy Spirit

The Day of Pentecost . . .
The Gathering of the Harvest

The "Day of Pentecost" was with the Israelites the great feast of the harvest, or "day of the first fruits," as told in Exodus 23:16 and Numbers 28:26.

> *Three times thou shalt keep a feast unto Me in the year . . . and the feast of the harvest, the first fruits of thy labours: and the feast of the gathering . . .*

> *Also in the day of the first fruits . . . ye shall have an Holy Convocation . . .*

Pentecost was celebrated on the fiftieth day after the Passover, which was ten days after the Ascension of Jesus. The Disciples, together with Matthias, who had been chosen to replace Judas (Acts 1:26), were in the upper room in Jerusalem observing the Jewish Festival when they received this outpouring of power. Matthias represents the lifting up of the life faculty, "given wholly to God."

We read about this baptism of power from God, of the Holy Spirit, in Acts 2:1-4

And when the Day of Pentecost was fully come, they were all with one accord in one place.

And suddenly there came a sound from heaven as of a rushing mighty wind, and it filled all the house where they were sitting.

And there appeared unto them, cloven tongues like as of fire, and it sat upon each of them.

And they were all filled with the Holy Spirit, and began to speak 'other tongues as the Spirit gave them utterance.'

The metaphysical meaning of the "Day of Pentecost" (the fiftieth day) is that in the unfoldment of the Spiritual Mind, there are periods when the ideas that we have meditated on, and accepted as true, become living realities in our life instead of mental concepts. In this awakening we get the "fruits of the ideas" that we have planted in our mind.

We have a direct, purposeful experience, and signs follow. Money follows a feeling of success and prosperity, an acceptance of and a "confessing with my mouth" that "all the Father hath is mine." I AM prosperous! The love object (person) follows the feeling, the accepting, and the "confessing with my mouth" that I AM (God in me is) loved and loving. Health follows the feeling, the accepting, and the "confessing with my mouth" attitude of Joy and the Allness of God as my life now. When we are awakened to Spiritual reality, the "Day of Pentecost" is the receiving of the Spirit as substance, as manifest on earth. *On earth as it is in heaven.* Matthew 6:9

They were all together in one place, means the concentration of all the faculties (disciples) and activities of the mind and body in acknowledgment and praise of Spirit. The result of this concentration is that the ordinary thinking mind and the perfect Christ mind blend and there is a descent of Spiritual energies (the Holy Spirit) into the body, *"it filled the house."*

When we are gathered in the upper chamber (a place of high spiritual understanding) and are unified in thought and purpose, "in one accord," we receive the gift of gifts—the Baptism of the Holy Spirit.

It seemed to the group of disciples that living tongues of fire played upon the head of every person present, uniting them and giving them a sense of power and confidence. *And began to speak with other tongues as the spirit gave them utterance.* When we are filled with the Holy Spirit, we do speak with other tongues, as the Spirit gives us utterance. There is no criticism; there is no condemnation, no self-judgment. We are very aware of what we say and of how we say it.

> *But ye shall receive power, after that the Holy Spirit is come upon you . . .*   Acts 1:8

Holy Spirit really means holy or sacred breath, the Breath of God, the Breath of Creation, by which all things are made. When this Breath of Creative Fire touches us, we are instantly galvanized into creative activity, inspired in some way according to our particular talent. Jesus the Christ never entered upon the ministry for which He came into this world until He was baptized with the Holy Spirit.

The Fruit of the Spirit, as detailed in Galatians 5:22 & 23 is: love, joy, peace, patience, kindness, goodness, fidelity, gentleness and temperance. These are the qualities that we are to outpicture in our lives. If the Fruit of the Spirit is evident in our life, then we may "love God and do as we please," as St. Augustine wrote. In this we find total freedom. *Against such there is no Law*, Galatians 5:23

The Fruit of the Spirit should be characteristic of each one of us. But the gifts of the Spirit are different. Every believer should have the same fruit as every other believer; but will have different gifts. God takes a talent and transforms it by the power of the Holy Spirit, to be used as s Spiritual Gift.

The Holy Spirit Baptism is not for the purpose of cleansing, but for the purpose of empowering for service. This empowering will not manifest itself in exactly the same way in each person. This is stated very clearly in I Corinthians 12:4, 12:8–11

Now there are diversities of gifts, but the same spirit . . .

For to one is given through the Spirit the Word of Wisdom;

To another the Word of Knowledge by the same spirit;

To another Faith by the same spirit;

To another the working of miracles;

To another prophecy;

To another discerning of spirits;

To another divers kinds of tongues;

To another interpretation of tongues;

But all these worketh that one and the selfsame spirit, dividing to every man severally as he will.

As we allow the Holy Spirit to direct us in the use of our gifts, we are empowered in their use. They could become a source of pride, therefore harm, if not used for His glory. In the Biblical sense, a gift of the Spirit means a "Gift of Holy Grace." When we are "commissioned" with a "Gift of Holy Grace," we are held accountable.

By God's grace, we have with us our helper, the Spirit of the Christ, the Holy Spirit, the Paraclete. "Paraclete" means "a helper called to one's side," an advocate, one who pleads another's cause. When Jesus the Christ told His disciples that He would shortly leave them and go to His Father He said:

And I will pray the Father and He shall give you another comforter (Paraclete) that he may abide with you forever:

Even the spirit of truth whom the world cannot receive because it seeth Him not, neither knoweth Him: But ye know Him: For He Dwelleth with you, and shall be in you.   John 14:16

"Another Comforter" was the phrase the Master used when giving to His disciples the promise of His abiding Spiritual Presence. He declared that His Spirit would be for them "another Comforter."

Jesus continues, John 14:26

But the Comforter (Paraclete) which is the Holy Spirit whom the Father will send in My name, He

*shall teach you all things, and bring all things to
your remembrance whatsoever I have said unto
you.*

Another interesting mention of the coming of the
promised Comforter is made in Chapter 16:7, where
Jesus says:

*Nevertheless, I tell you the truth! It is expedient
for you that I go away: For if I go not away, the
Comforter will not come unto you, but if I depart,
I will send Him unto you.*

Here, it is made very clear that the coming of the
Holy Spirit to the Disciples after the departure of Jesus
is to give them that inspiration and strength from
within, which they could not get as long as they relied
on Him who was with them.

With each person, there is always present an unseen
Divine Person whose loving presence is a *"Very present
help."* Psalm 46:1

Ernest Holmes writes in *Your Invisible Power*:
"You have a Friend within you who is closer than
your shadow. This Friend within you is infinite, since
He is a personification of God. He is at all times radi-
ant, free and happy. He is your inner, absolute and perfect Self.

The Friend within you is continously looking after your well-being. This Friend is a luminous Presence, evermore emerging from pure Spirit. He is the High Counselor, the Eternal Guide.

Possibly it will be difficult for you to believe that there is such a friend, but he is there at the very center of your being. He who keeps silent watch within you, lifts your consciousness to the realization that you are forever protected, forever safe, forever perfect.''

The Bible gives us definite instruction on how to receive the Holy Spirit. We first present ourselves to God in an act of surrender.

I beseech you therefore, brethren, by the mercies of God, that ye sacrifice, holy, acceptable unto God, which is your reasonable service.

And be not conformed to this world: But be ye transformed by the renewing of your mind, that ye may prove what is that good and acceptable, and perfect will of God.   Romans 12:1, 2

Those who would be used by the Spirit of Christ must live in accordance with the ''perfect will of God.'' As we awaken each morning and yield ourselves to the service of God, we should expect Him to keep us, guide us, and strengthen us to do His Holy Will.

The second step is to ask, Luke 11:9–13

And I say unto you, ask and it shall be given you: Seek, and ye shall find: Knock, and it shall be opened unto you. For everyone that asketh receiveth: and he that seeketh findeth: And to him that knocketh it shall be opened:

If a son shall ask bread of any of you that is a father, will he give him a stone? Or if he ask a fish, will he for a fish give him a serpent? Or if he ask an egg, will he offer him a scorpion?

If ye then, being evil, know how to give good gifts unto your children, how much more shall your heavenly Father give the Holy Spirit to them that ask him?

Ask of Me, and I will give thee, is always God's order. So we must ask. We open ourselves to the infilling of the Holy Spirit when we ask. We give our consent.

''God,'' said St. Augustine, ''who made us without our help will not save us without our consent.''

Acts 5:32 tells us the third step to take:

And we are His witnesses of these things: And so is also the Holy Spirit, whom God hath given to them that obey Him.

Obedience is quite as necessary as trust. We do not need more of the Spirit of Christ; we need to let the Spirit of Christ have more of us.

We are also told to live by faith.

This only would I learn of you, received ye the Spirit by the works of the Law, or by the hearing of Faith? The just shall live by Faith. Galatians 3:2

The Holy Spirit comes as a gift of God to us as we surrender ourselves to His Will, when we ask for the infilling and we are obedient. We accept this in faith. Faith is acting on our belief. We act on that truth and live with the full assurance that God has already filled us. In our hearts we give grateful thanks that this is done, accomplished, complete. God in action in the hearts and minds of each one of us is the Holy Spirit, the activity of God in our lives.

The Trinity defines God as Father, Son, and Holy Spirit. When we think of God as Father, we think of the creative will of the universe.

When we think of God's attempt to speak to man in history, we remember that God's love shone forth more clearly in Jesus of Nazareth than it has in any man that ever trod the earth. The Christ in Jesus and in each one of us is the only begotten of the Father. So

God as Love is the Son. We are the sons and daughters of God, the visible manifestation of God's love.

When we speak of the Spiritual Presence and of its creative activity, then we speak of the Holy Spirit. God the Father, God the Son, and God the Holy Spirit are One God.

There is but one Holy Spirit in this universe. Yet in that creative activity, we can see God the Holy Spirit or God the Eternal Mother, according to the way in which we look at it.

When we think of the sunlight, we think of one definite reality. We can look upon that sunlight as radiating forth from the sun, and we can also look upon it as being received by the earth, warming all, causing growth. Yet it is the same sunlight in both cases. The sunlight going forth from the sun may be compared to the Creative Activity as God the Holy Spirit. On the other hand, that same sunlight being received by the earth might symbolize the feminine side of creation, the Eternal Mother.

Fatherhood or Motherhood, Holy Spirit or Eternal Mother, are ways of looking at and experiencing the creative activity of God.

We experience God the Creator not as Father and Mother, but as One Being, Father-Mother, one Reality which can be experienced two different ways. Every one of us is father-mother, and it is only when we are both that we can be truly creative.

In all creative activity, we can experience both the creative force or masculine aspect, and the productivity or feminine aspect. The process of fermentation is the Eternal Mother, that of inspiration is the Holy Spirit.

The Day of Pentecost continues still. We are living in that privileged, wondrous day. We are living in the Age of the Holy Spirit. That for which the Disciples waited has been accomplished. The Day of Pentecost has fully come. The raised-up Christ consciousness is always within us, waiting only to be recognized. The God within us says, *This is my beloved child, in whom I am well pleased!* Matthew 3:17

The Bible was written by men with Spiritually illumined minds, and we can understand their words only as Divine Intelligence illumines our minds. *Let there be Light* (Genesis 1:3) This command is obeyed as we turn to the Divine Intelligence active in us. Whenever we open the Bible, we should affirm, *let there be light*, and close it with the grateful acknowledgment, *and there was light*. By this affirmation and acknowledgment, we attune our minds to the Spirit of Truth. No longer do we read the Bible and find it difficult to understand.

By studying the doctrines of the Atonement, the Resurrection, and the Ascension, we reach the truths unfolded in the inner mysteries, and we begin to understand the full truth of the teaching, that Jesus the Christ was not a unique personality, but *THE FIRST FRUITS OF THEM THAT SLEPT*. I Corinthians 15:20

In this way, Christ is not regarded as an "external Saviour," by whose righteousness we were to be saved from divine wrath, but the "First Fruits" of humanity, the model for each of us, which is *CHRIST IN YOU THE HOPE OF GLORY!* Colossians 1:27

Not to be saved by an external Christ, but to be glorified by an inner Christ, is the inner teaching of Christianity. We are to bear witness to the Christ within in everything we do, in everything we feel, and in everything we think and say until *That which is perfect is come, and that which is in part shall be done away.* I Corinthians 13:10

Such is the Transformational Journey as told in the Christ Story, lived through the Mysteries of old and now, and dramatically portrayed in symbols and allegory.

Bibliography

Bailes, Dr. Frederick, HIDDEN POWER FOR HUMAN PROBLEMS, Prentice-Hall, Englewood Cliffs, N.J.

Bailey, Alice A., FROM BETHLEHEM TO CALVARY, Lucis Publishing Trust, New York, N.Y.

Bailey, Alice A., THE RAYS AND THE INITIATIONS, Lucis Publishing Trust, New York, N.Y.

Besant, Annie, ESOTERIC CHRISTIANITY, The Theosophical Publishing House, Wheaton, Ill.

Blackwelder, Boyce W., LIGHT FROM THE GREEK NEW TESTAMENT, The Warner Press, Anderson, Ind.

Fillmore, Charles, THE TWELVE POWERS OF MAN, Unity School of Christianity, Lee's Summit, Mo.

Fosdick, Harry Emerson, A GUIDE TO UNDERSTANDING THE BIBLE, Harper & Row Publishers, New York, N.Y.

Gibran, Kahlil, THE PROPHET, Alfred A. Knopf, New York, N.Y.

Hall, Manly P., THE SECRET TEACHING OF ALL AGES, The Philosophical Research Society, Inc., Los Angeles, Calif.

Heindel, Max, ANCIENT AND MODERN INITIATION, L & N Fowler Co., Essex, England.

Holmes, Ernest, THE SCIENCE OF MIND, Dodd, Mead and Company, New York, N.Y.

Holmes, Ernest, YOUR INVISIBLE POWER, Science of Mind Publications, Los Angeles, Calif.

Phillips, Dorthy Berkely, edited by, THE CHOICE IS ALWAYS OURS, Theosophical Publishing House, Wheaton, Ill.

Nicoll, Maurice, THE MARK, Shambhala, Boulder, Co.

Seidenspinner, Clarence, GREAT PROTESTANT FESTIVALS, Henry Schuman, New York, N.Y.

Troward, Thomas, BIBLE MYSTERY AND BIBLE MEANING, Dodd, Mead & Company, New York, N.Y.

METAPHYSICAL BIBLE DICTIONARY, Unity School of Christianity, Lee's Summitt, Mo.

THE HOLY BIBLE, King James Version, Thomas Nelson, Inc., Nashville, Tenn.

THE INTERPRETERS' BIBLE, Abingdon, Nashville, Tenn.

THE INTERPRETERS' DICTIONARY OF THE BIBLE, Abingdon, Nashvile, Tenn.

THE SCOFIELD REFERENCE BIBLE, Oxford University Press, New York, N.Y.